THE GREAT LIVES SERIES

Great Lives biographies shed an exciting new light on the many dynamic men and women whose actions, visions, and dedication to an ideal have influenced the course of history. Their ambitions, dreams, successes and failures, the controversies they faced and the obstacles they overcame are the true stories behind these distinguished world leaders, explorers, and great Americans.

Other biographies in the Great Lives Series

CLARA BARTON: Founder of the American Red Cross
CHRISTOPHER COLUMBUS: The Intrepid Mariner
AMELIA EARHART: Challenging the Skies
THOMAS EDISON: Inventing the Future
JOHN GLENN: Space Pioneer
MIKHAIL GORBACHEV: The Soviet Innovator
JESSE JACKSON: A Voice for Change
JOHN F. KENNEDY: Courage in Crisis
MARTIN LUTHER KING: Dreams for a Nation
ABRAHAM LINCOLN: The Freedom President
NELSON MANDELA: A Voice Set Free
SALLY RIDE: Shooting for the Stars
FRANKLIN D. ROOSEVELT: The People's President
HARRIET TUBMAN: Call to Freedom

ACKNOWLEDGMENT

A special thanks to educators Dr. Frank Moretti, Ph.D., Associate Headmaster of the Dalton School in New York City; Dr. Paul Mattingly, Ph.D., Professor of History at New York University; and Barbara Smith, M.S., Assistant Superintendent of the Los Angeles Unified School District, for their contributions to the Great Lives Series.

GREAT LIVES

GOLDA MEIR
A Leader in Peace and War

Richard Amdur

FAWCETT COLUMBINE
NEW YORK

TABLE OF CONTENTS

Chapter 1
Mission Improbable   1
Chapter 2
Escape from the Pale   7
Chapter 3
Milwaukee   17
Chapter 4
A Taste of Freedom   25
Chapter 5
The Pioneering Life   33
Chapter 6
The Wretched Years   45
Chapter 7
A State Is Born   57
Chapter 8
Ambassador and Labor Minister   75
Chapter 9
On the World Stage   85
Chapter 10
Prime Minister Meir   95
Chapter 11
The Yom Kippur War   107

Glossary   118

Bibliography   121

1

Mission Improbable

A SHORT, NERVOUS WOMAN named Golda Meyerson looked out over the audience gathered before her. She had journeyed thousands of miles to a Chicago meeting hall, and now it was time for her to speak. The last few guests took their seats. Conversations came to a halt. Expectant faces turned toward her, as if to judge her before she even said a word. Golda realized that the warning she had been given earlier was true. This would be a tough audience.

"My friends," she began, "we are at war. There is no Jew in Palestine who does not believe that finally we will be victorious. That is the spirit of the country . . . However, this valiant spirit alone cannot face rifles and machine guns. Rifles and machine guns without spirit are not worth very much, but spirit without arms can, in time, be broken together with the body . . . ."

It was January 1948, and Golda had come to the United States from Palestine on a life-or-death mission. Jewish settlers there expected her to return home with millions of dollars in donations! They needed the money to buy weapons, and they needed it fast — within weeks — for it to make any difference. Less than three years after the end of World War II, during which six million Jews had been exterminated in the Holocaust, the Jews faced war with the Arabs for the right to live in the Middle East.

Golda Meyerson was doing her part to avoid yet another catastrophe for her people.

The Jews in Palestine, numbering 650,000, had ties to the land dating back to Biblical times. Since the late nineteenth century they had been reasserting their claim, and working toward the creation of an independent Jewish state.

The Arabs, numbering 1.2 million, also had ties to Palestine dating back many hundreds of years. They resisted the "newcomers," and called for a united Arab effort against them. The Arabs in Palestine also wanted a state of their own. Although the country was controlled by the British Army, Jews and Arabs were locked in an increasingly violent confrontation over who had the right to live there.

The British government had ruled Palestine since 1921. In 1947, faced with increasing violence and no obvious solution, it turned the problem over to the United Nations and announced its intention to take all British soldiers and other personnel out of Palestine by May 1948. In November 1947, the UN voted to "partition" the land into two states — one Jewish, one Arab. The Jews accepted the plan. Arabs rejected it. As the time left before the British withdrawal ran out, both sides tried to gain control of important roads and villages. Armed skirmishes happened every day. Full-fledged war was considered inevitable, and the Jews were terrified.

The Arab soldiers greatly outnumbered the Jewish soldiers, 50,000 to 3,000. The Arabs also had artillery, armored vehicles, and an air force. The Jews had no tanks, no airplanes, and an assortment of very old firearms. They needed to buy new weapons — and for that they needed a lot of money.

David Ben-Gurion was the leader of the Jewish community in Palestine — called the *Yishuv* or settlement in the Hebrew language. He thought he should do the fund-raising himself. At an important meeting in Tel Aviv, his aides convinced him that Golda Meyerson should do it instead.

Golda had also been a leader in the Yishuv for many years. She had also spent much of her childhood in Milwaukee and was fluent in English. Golda had already traveled throughout America on behalf of Palestinian Jewish organizations, and knew the country well. She had a good record when it came to getting American Jews to open their wallets. But most of all, the formidable Ben-Gurion was needed in Palestine during the time of terrible crisis.

Ben-Gurion agreed that it made more sense for Golda to make the trip. Still, that didn't mean he and other Jewish leaders expected her to succeed. On the contrary, American Jews had already been extremely generous. No one knew if they would be in the mood to give more.

After meeting with Ben-Gurion, Golda accepted the assignment. She headed straight to the airport in Tel Aviv, without even stopping at home to pack. She boarded the plane and a few days later arrived in Chicago, without any luggage and still wearing the same dress and winter coat!

Golda's sister, Clara, lived in Chicago and worked for the Council of Jewish Federations and Welfare Funds. She had arranged for Golda's first speech, to a group of professional fund-raisers at the organization's General Assembly. Finally, the time had come. Standing at the podium, Golda fixed a steady gaze upon an audience of people she did not know but whose help she needed desperately.

Because she was a gifted speaker, and able to "read" her audience, she sensed that her words needed to be especially persuasive. In earlier fund-raising speeches, Golda told heroic tales of the brave settlers in Palestine, working to build a Jewish state. These were sturdy pioneers, she would say, who were strong and resourceful enough to withstand any challenge, even the combined might of the Arab states that surrounded Palestine.

But on this evening, Golda decided against giving that speech. The Jews needed help badly. She had left behind a dire situation in Palestine. When it came to the survival of her people, she could not mince her words. She felt that if she could cope with the full truth, so could her audience.

The audience listened with rapt attention as Golda spoke movingly of the tinderbox that was Palestine.

"Our problem," Golda continued, "is time. The question is what can we get immediately. And, when I say immediately, this does not mean next month. It does not mean two months from now. It means now . . . ."

4

Reaching the most difficult part of her speech, she made her plea to the Chicago crowd:

"I have come here to try to impress Jews in the United States with the fact that within a very short period, a couple of weeks, we must have in cash between twenty-five and thirty million dollars . . . . I know that we are not asking for something easy, I know that collecting at once a sum such as I ask is not simple . . . ."

Golda's voice filled the quiet hall with descriptions of the sacrifices made by the Jews of Palestine — people who stood on line for hours just to donate blood for wounded Jewish fighters, others who pitched in any way they could. The implication for the Jews of America was clear — they *had* to contribute.

Golda ended her speech with a final, emotional appeal:

"You cannot decide whether we should fight or not. We will . . . . That decision is taken. Nobody can change it. You can only decide one thing: whether we shall be victorious in this fight . . . . That decision American Jews can make. It has to be made quickly, within hours, within days. And I beg of you — don't be too late. Don't be bitterly sorry three months from now for what you failed to do today. The time is now."

People in her audience first began to weep. The Jews of Palestine were in need, and Golda had dramatically and effectively conveyed what that need meant. Then they opened their wallets and pocketbooks and gave money — the millions of dollars that Golda had asked for.

Golda toured the country for the next six weeks and the reaction was the same wherever she spoke. Jews all over America heard her words and responded. Some even took out loans in order to give money! When all was said and done, Golda had raised the astonishing sum of $50 million!

Waiting anxiously in Tel Aviv, Ben-Gurion was thrilled. Golda had kept him informed of her progress through her mission. Upon her return he greeted her at the airport and hailed her as a savior.

"Someday," he said, "when history will be written, it will be said that there was a Jewish woman who got the money which made the state possible."

Ben-Gurion was right. Thanks in large part to the money Golda raised on her journey to the United States, the Jews were able to strengthen their forces at a crucial stage of the struggle with the Arabs. In May 1948 they prevailed in a war of independence and established the state of Israel. For Golda Meyerson, who later changed her name to Meir from the Hebrew word meaning "to illuminate," this was as it should be. From childhood she had known that the Jews could never rest easy until they had a country they called their own.

2

Escape from the Pale

GOLDA WAS BORN on May 3, 1898, the seventh child of Moshe and Blume Mabovitch, but only the second to live through infancy. The family lived in the Russian city of Kiev, about 500 miles south of Moscow. They were poor, as were most Jews of the time. There was never enough heat, warm clothing, or food. Golda was often so hungry that she resented having to share her food — little more than gruel — with Clara, her baby sister. Her older sister, Sheyna, was often so weak that she fainted in school.

The Mabovitches were discriminated against because they were Jewish. Moshe was a skilled carpenter and cabinet maker. Often, when his customers discovered he was Jewish, they refused to pay him. Russian law offered no protection. In fact, it did just the opposite — it legalized prejudice toward Jews.

Most of Russia's Jews were forced to live in a region along the country's western frontier known as the Pale of Settlement. (The word "pale" is a noun meaning an area defined by certain boundaries. Since the days of the Pale of Settlement, the phrase "beyond the pale" has come into use. It means an action or behavior that most people consider outside of what is civilized.)

About five million Jews lived in poverty in the Pale of Settlement. They also faced the constant threat of persecution and massacres, known as pogroms, which were carried out by Russian soldiers and citizens alike. One such massacre occurred in 1881, when a Jew was among the conspirators who assinated the tsar of Russia, Alexander II. The murder also led to the creation of the May Laws, regulations that limited the types of jobs and education Jews could have, and where they could live.

Another pogrom occurred in 1903 at Kishinev, where forty-five Jews were killed and more than a thousand Jewish homes and shops were looted or destroyed. Upon hearing the news of Kishinev, Jews throughout the Pale staged protests. Many fasted in memory of the Kishinev dead. Although she was just five years old, Golda insisted on joining the fast, against the wishes of her parents who already worried whether she was getting enough to eat.

Another time, when Golda was three or four years old, a rumor swept through Kiev that a pogrom was about to occur. Cossacks, or Russian cavalry troops, had gone on a rampage elsewhere in the city, it was said, and were heading toward the Mabovitches' neighborhood, looking for Jews.

As the day grew dark, Moshe burst into the house carrying several wooden boards and a handful of nails. With the help of a man who lived upstairs, he worked furiously to cover up the windows and the doors. Golda, perched on the stairs, watched in horror. It was a crude defense, for surely the burly Cossacks and their horses could break through if they wanted to. But it was all the family could do. Moshe gathered his wife and children around him, and waited for the terror to pass.

Though no pogrom occurred, the incident haunted Golda for her entire life. As she later wrote, "The pogrom was against Jews — it was against me . . . . I was Jewish, and different from all the other children in the yard. There was no pogrom against them. Their fathers were not nailing boards to the door — only my father . . . ."

The event was also a stark reminder of the awful situation in which Jews everywhere lived. They were defenseless, helpless before the power of hostile governments and citizens. It was a situation that had to change.

The sorry state of the Jews in nineteenth-century Russia was hardly unique, either for the time or in history. Indeed, the Pale of Settlement and the May Laws were only the latest examples of "anti-Semitism." Anti-Semitism is discrimination against Jews because of their religion.

Anti-Semitism was widespread in Europe throughout the Middle Ages, from the late fifth through the fifteenth century. Jews were scorned and persecuted by Christians, who held them responsible for the crucifixion of Jesus Christ. Beginning in the eleventh century, a wave of massacres against the Jews were committed in the name of the Crusades. These were a series of Christian military expeditions from Europe to the Middle East that sought to oust the Muslim "infidels" from the Holy

Land, which is what Christians called the region where Jesus had lived. Heightened religious passions left little room for tolerance of people of other religious beliefs.

The Spanish Inquisition, established in 1478 by King Ferdinand and Queen Isabella' of Spain, also led to extreme acts of violence against Jews. The Inquisition was an intensely violent campaign against people who did not agree with the religious ideas of the Catholic church.

Hatred of Jews also grew out of their visible role in Spanish society. Many had become financiers who were highly influential with the Spanish royals. As such they proved an easy scapegoat for people angry at high taxes and poverty in general. Anti-Semitism plagued Germany, Poland, and Russia throughout the ensuing centuries for many of the same reasons.

The pogrom and massacre of Jews that took place in Kishinev, therefore, was no surprise, as devastating as it was for those who perished or who were left homeless. It may even have brought a sense of urgency to people like Moshe Mabovitch, who had heard about a "golden land" where opportunity abounded and where an honest man could work hard and prosper. That land was America. Moshe decided to try his luck there. He planned to return to Russia rich enough to greatly improve his family's life.

Moshe arrived first in New York City, but found jobs and a place to live very hard to find. He decided to continue on to Milwaukee, Wisconsin, in America's midwest. Many other European immigrants lived there, and there was a large Jewish community. There he rented a small apartment in a poor Jewish neighborhood, took a job as a carpenter for a railroad, and began to earn a living.

Moshe's departure for the United States meant that his wife and children could no longer live in the city of Kiev, because it was outside the Pale of Settlement. Moshe's skill as a carpenter had won the family special permission to live there. Now that he was gone, there was no reason for the authorities to be so "generous." Golda's mother Blume took her three daughters to her hometown, Pinsk, and moved in with Golda's grandfather.

Pinsk, located deep within the Pale of Settlement, was much smaller than Kiev. It was a major center of Jewish culture. Jews owned businesses and factories there, practiced their religion, and sent their children to Jewish schools. Pinsk was also the center of the *Hovevei Zion* which means "Lovers of Zion" in the Yiddish language. Yiddish is a mixture of German and Hebrew words, and is spoken by Jews from central Europe.

Hovevei Zion was one of several groups that had begun to send Jewish men and women to settle in Palestine. These pioneers were known as Zionists. Zion is the name given in the Old Testament of the Bible to the city of the Jewish King David. This city is more commonly called Jerusalem. The Zionists' goal was to establish a modern Jewish state in the land from which their ancestors had been expelled in biblical times.

Jews had dreamed of returning to the Holy Land for some 2,000 years, ever since the destruction of the second temple in Jerusalem, by Roman soldiers. The first temple was built by King Solomon in the tenth century

11

B.C. — almost 3,000 years ago. It served as the center of Jewish worship and of an empire that stretched throughout ancient Palestine. It borders included today's Israel and parts of Egypt, Jordan, Syria, Iraq, and Lebanon. Solomon's temple was totally destroyed in 586 B.C. by the Babylonians, whose dynasty was expanding and who had taken control of the area.

Most of the Jews were carted off to Babylonia to be used as slaves. The event created what is known as the Diaspora, which comes from a Greek word that means "scattering." Eventually, the ancient Jews returned to their land. They rebuilt Jerusalem and a second temple. However, in 70 A.D. the Romans destroyed it in a terrible war that ended Jewish power. Once again, the Jews were driven into exile. But ever since then, Jews have prayed to return to Jerusalem.

In the late nineteenth and early twentieth century, they began to do exactly that. They were following the lead of a Viennese journalist and lawyer by the name of Theodor Herzl. In 1896 Herzl published a pamphlet in German called *Der Judenstaat*, or *The Jewish State, An Attempt at a Modern Solution of the Jewish Question*. It grew out of Herzl's experiences with anti-Semitism in Vienna, and also out of an episode in France involving a Jewish army officer named Alfred Dreyfus.

The Dreyfus Affair, as it came to be called, startled the entire country, but it shocked the Jews. In the 1890s, Dreyfus was convicted of treason for passing military information to the Germans. He was condemned to life imprisonment on Devil's Island in French Guiana.

In 1906 a court set aside the Dreyfus decision as

"wrongful" and "erroneous," and acknowledged that the actions against Dreyfus could be traced to anti-Semitism. But by then the damage had been done. The Jews had thought that France was among the more advanced and liberal countries in Europe. If such obvious anti-Semitism existed here, they thought, Jews were not safe anywhere.

As Paris correspondent for a newspaper called the *Vienna Neue Freie Presse* — the Vienna New Free Press — Herzl had covered the Dreyfus Affair and witnessed mobs shouting "Death to the Jews" as part of the trial. He, too, realized that the only way that the Jews could ever hope to live in freedom and with dignity would be if they had a land of their own. *Der Judenstaat* was his call to action.

The reception to *Der Judenstaat* was mixed. Religious Jews, especially rabbis, opposed Herzl on theological grounds. They felt that a Jewish state would only occur with the coming of the messiah, and that to act otherwise was against fundamental Jewish religious principles. Many other Jews reacted with skepticism and apathy. How could the poor, powerless Jews ever hope to do something as grand as form a state?

But Jews from Eastern Europe — those who lived under the threat of pogroms and suffered the worst from anti-Semitism — were very positive about Herzl's plan. So were Zionist intellectuals, whose imaginations were fired by Herzl's daring and the zeal with which he put forth his ideas. Zionism, with its promises of justice for all, also appealed to large numbers of Jewish workers. In fact, so-called "Labor Zionism" would quickly become the main branch of Zionism and have a great in-

13

fluence on the Zionist movement's growth and development.

In 1897, after the publication of *Der Judenstaat*, Herzl called for the First Zionist Congress, in Basel, Switzerland. Herzl later declared, "At Basel I founded the Jewish State." A historic process had been catapulted into motion.

Zionism was one of the main topics of conversation at the tavern in Pinsk run by Golda's grandfather. There, Zionists, socialists, radicals, and others gathered to debate politics. They discussed, among other things, what all Russians — and especially Jews living in Russia — could do to make their lives better. Change was in the air. The older generation was somewhat resigned to living under the foot of the tsar, forever banished from their real homeland in Palestine. For instance, Golda's grandmother poured salt in her tea as a symbol to remind her of the bitter taste of living in the Diaspora.

But the younger generation was ready to take action. Golda's sister Sheyna had joined a Zionist Socialist group, which was forbidden by the Russian government. She had also fallen in love with Shamai Korngold, a fiery young leader of the local Zionist Socialists. Blume worried that Sheyna would be arrested, tortured, or even sent to the Russian wasteland of Siberia, a common punishment for troublemakers and criminals. Blume pleaded daily with Sheyna to end her Zionist activities, saying she would cause grave trouble for herself, her family, and even for her father in America. But Sheyna's resolve only grew stronger.

The police station next door to the Mabovitch household only aggravated Blume's concerns. Night after

14

night, the police brought in young socialists for questioning. They were tortured and beaten, and their horrible cries filled the night.

"It's she! It's she!" Blume would cry, thinking she recognized Sheyna's screams. For young Golda, it was a childhood punctuated by such noises — the police station screams, the shouting matches between Blume and Sheyna, and the ominous clop-clop-clop of the Cossacks' horses' hooves on the street outside her grandfather's house.

Blume worked at the tavern and also sold her home-baked bread to Jewish housewives in the neighborhood. Eventually she saved enough money to move the family into its own apartment. The Mabovitch girls were finally getting enough to eat. But Blume was feeling more and more desperate about the situation in Russia. In particular she worried about Sheyna's political actions. She wrote to Moshe, telling him that he must change his plans — he must bring the entire family to America instead of returning home. Moshe replied that he would send for the family as soon as he had saved enough money to pay their passage.

Finally, in 1906, the Mabovitch family departed. They traveled first by train and horse-drawn wagon across Russia, then Austria and Hungary (which was one big country at the time), and Germany, to Antwerp, Belgium, where a ship was waiting for them.

When Moshe had traveled to America, he had helped a friend's family to escape at the same time by using identity papers for the Mabovitch family. At the time, it didn't matter because Moshe thought he would be returning to Russia. Now that the rest of the real Ma-

15

bovitch family was traveling to America, they had to use false travel documents. The entire family had to memorize facts about their new "identities." For instance, eight-year-old Golda, according to these illicit papers, was supposed to be just five years old.

En route, Golda's mother had to pay bribes to border guards, and the whole family had to worry that the false travel documents they carried would be not discovered. To make matters worse, their luggage was lost. After a nerve-racking physical examination in Antwerp, Belgium — people could be turned away if they suffered even small ailments such as lice — the Mabovitches were allowed aboard ship.

The two-week ocean voyage was yet another hardship. The ship was crowded with hundreds of other poor, scared people leaving Europe for new lives in America. The accommodations, located deep in the hold of the ship, consisted of bunk beds with no mattresses or blankets. Golda was the only one in her family who didn't get seasick.

When she wasn't standing in line, waiting for food to be ladled out to her, Golda spent most of her time on deck, huddled against the wind, staring out to sea and wondering what life in Milwaukee would be like.

The ship arrived in Quebec, Canada, where the family boarded a train for Milwaukee. They were looking forward to a joyous reunion with Moshe. A new city, a new language, a new life — all this and more lay ahead.

3

Milwaukee

MILWAUKEE . . . OVERWHELMED ME: new food, the baffling sounds of an entirely unfamiliar language, the confusion of getting used to a parent I had almost forgotten. It all gave me a feeling of unreality so strong that I can still remember standing in the street and wondering who and where I was."

This is how Golda described her first moments in the United States when, many years later, she wrote about her life. Trolley cars, electric lights, running water — all of this was new to her. Even her father looked different. When the family was reunited on the railway platform, the three girls were startled by his clean-shaven face and the American-style clothing he wore. They had not seen Moshe for three years, and they couldn't help but wonder if this strange-looking man was really their father.

The very next day, Moshe took Golda and her sisters shopping at a Milwaukee department store to buy them some "American" clothing. For Golda, the excursion was also a thrilling adventure. The five-story building was the largest she had ever been in. And the bustle of modern Milwaukee was a dramatic change from the muddy streets of Pinsk.

Golda's new clothes made her look like a true American. Eight years old, she was a plain, tall girl whose outstanding feature was her hair — long, wavy, chestnut in color, and usually worn in thick, heavy braids. Childhood photographs show a girl not given to smiling, but one whose seriousness is readily apparent.

Sheyna, however, was not as willing to trade in her European past for the promise of America. Standing on principle — and still in mourning for Theodor Herzl, who had died in 1904 — she refused to wear the new clothing her father bought her, preferring instead her matronly black dress. This standoff was the first indication that the new life the Mabovitches were starting for themselves in the United States would soon feature many of the same tensions — over money, Zionism, and willful daughters — that been part of the household in Russia.

On occasion, more palpable ghosts from the Pale of Settlement made themselves evident — at least in the eyes of little Clara, the youngest. Shortly after their arrival in the United States, the family went to see Moshe march in the Labor Day parade. Moshe was proud to take part in this American tradition, and so was Golda. As she later wrote, "To see my father marching on that September day was like coming out of the dark into the light."

But Clara, seeing the mounted cavalry leading the workers on parade, remembered only the rampaging

Golda Meir as a young girl when her name was Golda Mabovitch. She was born in Kiev, Russia where her father was a poor Jewish carpenter. Life for the Mabovitch family didn't improve until they moved to Milwaukee, when Golda was eight years old.

horsemen in Russia, who had so often run roughshod over the little Jewish girls at play. "The Cossacks! The Cossacks are coming!" she cried in fear. She was so upset by the incident that she had to be taken home and put to bed.

After a few months in the small room Moshe had rented, the family settled into larger quarters — an apartment Blume had found in the first floor of a house in the city's Jewish neighborhood. Golda entered school as a second-grader, and took quickly to both her schoolwork and to the English language. Her mother decided to establish a small grocery store in the front room of the apartment. Although she intended it to help the family earn more money, it became another problem instead.

Moshe was a proud man and to him, having his wife run a grocery store meant that he didn't make enough money to support his family with his own work. In his eyes, it also wasn't right for a woman to work. In those days, most women were housewives, and didn't have jobs outside the home.

Sheyna thought that running a grocery made the family "social parasites" — they would be living off other people's needs. In keeping with her political ideas, she took a job at a factory and eventually moved out to support herself.

Golda, too, had her problems with the store. Forced to help out in the mornings, she was constantly late for school. Before long this attracted the attention of the school's truant officials. But more importantly, Golda herself was angry. She had quickly moved to the head of her class at the Fourth Street Elementary School, and she wanted nothing to interfere with her education.

A problem at school prompted Golda to undertake her first fund-raising activity — and her first appeal to people's hearts to do what was right. The Milwaukee school system required that everyone pay a small sum for textbooks. Upon hearing that some children couldn't afford this, Golda and a friend, Regina Hamburger, decided to do something about it.

Golda understood what it meant to be poor. Her family had been that way in Russia, and remained needy even in America. Golda's actions were also in the best tradition of Labor Zionism, even though her own Zionist consciousness had not yet developed.

Golda and her friend Regina founded the "American Young Sisters Society." With hand-made posters promising sandwiches and tea, they announced a program to be held on a Saturday night at an auditorium nine-year-old Golda had rented. Lots of people came. Clara recited a poem, and Golda gave a short speech about how everyone needed books, not just those who could afford them. When the evening was over, the satisfied girls found that they had collected more money than they had expected.

Education had come to mean everything to Golda. By the time she was about to enter high school, she had decided that she wanted to become a teacher. This worried her parents. They wanted her to work in the shop, or perhaps attend secretarial school. To them, education was a luxury for a young Jewish girl. Her father told her, "Young women should seek husbands, not

21

education . . . . It doesn't pay to be too clever. Men don't like smart girls."

Her parents' worries became more pronounced after an announcement by the Milwaukee school system that married women would not be hired as teachers. Thinking that her chosen career would condemn her to being an "old maid," her parents even went so far as to arrange a marriage for her — with a man more than twice her age! This was quite common among Jews in Russia, but Golda was horrified. She insisted on her desire to become a teacher.

Her older sister Sheyna encouraged her. Sheyna had been sent to a hospital in Denver, Colorado, to be treated for tuberculosis. She lived there with her old friend from Pinsk, Shamai, who had followed her first to Milwaukee and then to Denver. None of his Zionist passions had cooled. In fact, he had only recently escaped from prison after being arrested for making statements against Russia's tsar. He and Sheyna had married and set up a home in Denver.

Sheyna sent her letters to Golda's best friend Regina's house, so that they wouldn't be intercepted by their mother Blume. In one of them she wrote, "No, you shouldn't stop school. You are too young to work. You have a good chance to become something . . . . My advice is you should get ready and come to us. We are not rich either, but you will have good chances here to study and we will do all we can for you . . . . First, you'll have all the opportunities to study; second, you'll have plenty to eat; third, you'll have all the necessary clothes a person ought to have . . . ."

Golda was touched by the willingness of her sister

and Shamai to let her live with them. She also realized that she had to take control of her life if she was to do what she wanted. Her parents' desires for her were just too different from what she herself wanted to do. Living under the same roof with them would be tense, if not downright miserable. It was 1912. She was fourteen years old and about to enter high school. Golda decided to run away from home.

For several weeks she taught English to recent immigrants for ten cents an hour to earn the money she needed for the rail ticket to Denver. Regina helped her plan the actual "escape." She agreed to stash Golda's luggage the night before, so that Golda wouldn't attract notice when she left her house in the morning.

But even with all the girls' planning, Golda almost bungled the plan. She hadn't taken into account the simple fact that trains run according to a schedule — they're not just waiting there at the station. Even as her parents were reading the note she had left explaining her actions, Golda was waiting anxiously for the train. As Golda later wrote:

"I had considerably more luck than brains, and somehow or other, in the confusion, no one looked for me until the train had left and I was on my way to Sheyna . . . I had done something that deeply wounded my mother and father but that was truly essential for me."

The city of Denver would prove to be a lot of things for Golda. It was the place where she had her first taste of independence, her first boyfriend, and her first apartment. But most of all, she would see firsthand what it was that had fired up Sheyna's imagination for so long — the Zionist movement, up close and in action.

4

A Taste of Freedom

SHEYNA AND SHAMAI's Denver apartment had become a gathering place for a number of angry young intellectuals who had also gone for treatment of tuberculosis at the hospital. In discussions lasting well into the early hours of the morning, Golda heard them talk about injustice — against women, workers, and Jews. These fervent people called themselves Zionists, socialists, and anarchists.

As she listened, Golda also heard moving stories of the settlers in Palestine who were building a home for the Jews, and trying to create a country that would be free of all the ills that plagued the world. Golda was excited by what she heard, even more than she was by her schoolwork. Though she came to Denver without any strong political ideas, that changed quickly.

"I listened raptly to everyone holding forth, but it was to the Socialist-Zionists that I found myself listening most attentively, and it was their political philosophy that made the most sense to me. I understood and responded fully to the idea of a national home for the Jews

25

— one place on the face of the earth where Jews could be free and independent . . . . I was much more interested in the kind of Jewish national home the Zionists wanted to create in Palestine than I was in the political scene in Denver itself, or even in what was then going on in Russia."

In particular, Golda was drawn to the thinking of Aaron David (A.D.) Gordon and Eugene V. Debs, two men whose work was discussed in Denver. Debs was a labor leader and founder of the Socialist Party of America. Gordon has been called a "prophet of the religion of labor." Following his lead, many Zionists believed that Jewish dignity, self-esteem, and the power to control their own lives could be found by actually moving to Palestine and working the land. Gordon was not much for political theories and debates. He was a pacifist, which meant he did not believe in ever fighting a war, and he preached that the pioneers should be "zealots of labor."

Golda had an awakening of another sort in Denver. No longer a girl, Golda had grown into a tall woman whose beautiful hair and personal intensity attracted many suitors. Though she was surrounded by fiery young activists, it was someone on the outskirts of this crowd who attracted her attention.

Morris Meyerson was not an angry young intellectual. Rather, he was a quiet man. Meyerson, as he was known, was employed as a sign painter, but his true love was arts, especially music and literature. He gave Golda books to read and took her to concerts and recitals. Golda, thoroughly enjoying her "education," was taken by Meyerson's manner. In a letter to Regina she

26

wrote: "He isn't very handsome, but he has a beautiful soul."

Life in Denver was not all talk. Golda worked after school at Shamai's dry-cleaning establishment. Shamai in turn would go off to his second job as a part-time janitor at the local telephone company. But as the weeks and months wore on, life with Shamai and Sheyna eventually proved to be almost as difficult for Golda as it had been with her parents. Sheyna did not approve of Golda's spending so much time with Morris, nor with the other men Golda dated.

Golda had spent much of her life in awe of Sheyna. A woman of action and strong beliefs, Sheyna was an impressive role model. But Golda was determined to live the way she chose, and after one especially heated argument with her sister she stalked out of the Denver apartment. It was time for her to be on her own. After staying with friends for a short while, she found an apartment, dropped out of high school, and took a job at a department store selling dress linings and taking measurements for skirts.

In those days, a respectable Jewish girl was not supposed to have her own apartment or do such menial work. When her parents found out, they were horrified. It wasn't long before Golda received a letter from her father, begging her to return home. In it, Moshe promised not to interfere with her desire to continue her education and become a teacher.

In early 1914, after a little more than a year on her own, Golda returned to Milwaukee. Meyerson remained in Denver to care for his sister, but the two swore their love for each other and planned to resume

27

a life together as soon as possible. His letters, though, went to Regina's house — to avoid the suspicious gaze of Golda's protective mother.

Golda spent the next two years completing high school, and then enrolled in the Milwaukee Teachers' Training College. Her parents had moved to another apartment, which in ways came to resemble the bustle of Shamai's and Sheyna's in Denver. Moshe had become involved in Jewish community work, and the Mabovitch household had become a transit post for Zionists visiting Milwaukee.

Among those visitors were recruiters from Palestine. They were looking for new members of a "Jewish Legion," an all-Jewish force that would be part of the British Army and would help fight in World War I, which had broken out that year. The war looked as if it would determine the fate of Palestine, since the Turks who controlled Palestine were fighting against the British. The Jews wanted to help the British defeat the Turks. So did Golda, who was disappointed to learn that the Jewish Legion was for men only.

There was, however, another outlet for Golda's Jewish passions. While working as a librarian at the local library, she also taught part-time at a local Yiddish school. Many Jewish immigrants from Russia and Eastern Europe, where Yiddish was the day-to-day language, continued to speak Yiddish in America. She spoke out in public about Zionism, and about the continued discrimination against Jews in Europe.

Her father, though he agreed with what she was saying, did not want his daughter doing something as unladylike as speaking on street corners. He threatened to drag her home by her braided hair if he caught her. Later, he happened to hear her speak and he took back his angry words.

In 1915, Golda had joined the local chapter of Poale Zion. "Poale" is the Yiddish word for worker, and Poale Zion was an organization for men and women who wanted to actually live in Palestine. But this move also set her on a collision course with her boyfriend, Morris.

Morris Meyerson had joined Golda in Milwaukee. But the joy of their reunion was tempered by their disagreement over Palestine. Morris simply didn't care at all for Zionism or the efforts to resurrect the Jewish state. As he wrote in one letter: "I don't know whether to be glad or sorry that you seem to be so enthusiastic a nationalist. I am altogether passive in this matter, though I give you full credit for your activity, as I do all others engaged in doing something toward helping a distressed nation . . . . But . . . I do not care particularly as to whether the Jews are going to suffer in Russia or in the Holy Land."

In another he wrote, "The idea of Palestine or any other territory for Jews is to me ridiculous. Racial persecution does not exist because some nations have no territories, but because nations exist at all."

In 1916 the Chicago branch of Poale Zion asked Golda to move to Chicago, where they felt her talents could better serve the organization. Golda decided to go along, and soon found herself living with the family of B.J. and Raziel Shapiro. She found part-time work at the Chicago Public Library, and became close friends with Raziel. Her sister Sheyna, brother-in-law Shamai, and best friend Regina, as well as other friends, had all moved to Chicago, and Golda saw them often. But she was not happy being away from Morris, nor about the choice she faced — between marrying Morris or going to live in Palestine. She returned to Milwaukee to be close to Morris, and to her surprise, she found him more receptive to the idea of moving to Palestine.

As World War I drew to a close, the British had defeated the Turkish Army and taken control of Palestine. On November 2, 1917, Britain issued a paper called the Balfour Declaration, which declared that it might be possible for Jews in Palestine to have their own homeland. For the first time in history, the government of a powerful country supported the Zionist goal. Suddenly, the dreams of idealistic Zionists such as Golda, and of the settlers in Palestine, did not seem so unrealistic after all.

Less than two months later, on December 24, 1917, Morris and Golda were married in a traditional wedding ceremony. However, they could not move to Palestine right away. World War I was still raging, and they needed to save money for the long trip. But the plan was made.

Golda's work for Poale Zion became even more important. She traveled around the United States and to Canada on behalf of the organization. Her parents were surprised that a young wife would leave her new husband, but Morris understood how important Golda's work was, and she wrote to him often. Golda succeeded in raising money and founding new Poale Zion chapters in other cities. Fluent in both Yiddish and English, she became one of Poale Zion's most popular speakers.

In the winter of 1918 the first convention of the American Jewish Congress was held in Philadelphia, Pennsylvania. It was an event that convinced her, the delegate from Milwaukee, that she was on the right track with her life's work. Years later she wrote, "When journalists ask me when my political career actually began, my mind always flashes back to that convention, to the smoke-filled hall in a Philadelphia hotel where I sat for hours listening, completely absorbed, to the details of the program being thrashed out; to the excitement of the debates and of being able to cast my own vote."

Two years later, Golda and Morris Meyerson finally prepared to move to Palestine. They sold their furniture, curtains, and other belongings, even their winter clothing — not knowing that winter in the desert can be harsh. About the only thing they kept was Morris's phonograph and their record collection.

Stopping in Chicago on their way to New York City, from which the ship to Palestine would sail, they made a farewell visit to Shamai and Sheyna. Golda spoke excitedly to her sister about the journey she was about to make and the new lives they were beginning in Palestine. Jokingly, Shamai said to Sheyna, "Maybe you'd like to go, too?"

To everyone's astonishment, Sheyna replied "Yes!" and began packing her bags! Three weeks later, Golda, her husband, her sister Sheyna, and several other friends set sail aboard the S.S. *Pocahontas*, dreaming of a new life in Palestine. Shamai would remain in the United States for several years before joining Sheyna and the others.

Awaiting them in the Middle East was a region on the brink of historic change. World War I had led to the complete dissolution of the Ottoman Empire, as British and French forces drove the Turks out. Great Britain took over the administration of Palestine — and quickly found itself caught in the middle of another potentially violent international conflict.

Britain's Balfour Declaration committed it to allowing Jewish emigration to Palestine in large numbers, the establishment of Hebrew as an official language, along with English and Arabic, and the formation of a Jewish Agency that would help Jews build a national homeland.

At the same time, Arab nationalism was becoming very strong. Arabs greatly outnumbered the Jews — in 1922, there were about 80,000 Jews in Palestine, only eleven percent of the population. In addition, the Arabs had helped the British during World War I, and felt they were owed something in return.

The conflict between the two communities deepened. Full-scale Arab riots had erupted to protest the increased numbers of Jews in the country. The British were caught in a dilemma. If they fulfilled their promises to the Jews, they would make enemies of the entire Arab world. But how could they go back on their word to the Jews, as written in the Balfour Declaration? And most of all, until they came up with a solution to the problem, how would the British keep the peace?

5

The Pioneering Life

JUST ABOUT EVERYTHING that could go wrong with Golda's journey to Palestine, did. The good ship *Pocahontas* proved to be a remarkably unseaworthy vessel. There were constant engine problems and even fires. Worse yet was the crew. Protesting the poor conditions in general, they staged a mutiny the first day out, and several of the unruly crewmen were thrown in the ship's brig.

The captain's brother went mad and had to be locked in his cabin for the duration of the voyage. The captain himself later turned up dead, either murdered or a suicide. What crew remained to run the ship took out their anger on the passengers. Among other things, they mixed sea water with the regular supply of drinking water. Three of the people who traveled with Golda ended their trip in Boston, the ship's first stop.

Somehow, the ship made it to Naples, Italy. There, Golda and the others switched to another ship that was to take them to Alexandria, Egypt. This leg of the voyage presented them with another problem. Among their traveling companions was a group of Lithuanians also making their way to Palestine. Because they couldn't afford cabins, they slept outdoors on the deck of the ship.

The Lithuanians had worked on training farms in Europe as part of their preparations for working the land in Israel. They considered themselves superior to the "soft, pampered" American Zionists, who were able to sleep snugly in cabins below deck. Golda decided to show the Lithuanians that she and her fellow Americans were just as sturdy and rugged as they. She convinced her traveling party to give up their cabins and sleep on deck too. Golda made her point — never mind that now everyone was uncomfortable, and that perhaps even the Lithuanians might have preferred cabins.

From Alexandria it was necessary to take a train, cross the Suez Canal, travel through the northern part of the Sinai Peninsula and along the coast of the Mediterranean to reach their destination — Tel Aviv. Tel Aviv was a new Jewish city that had risen next to the Arab port city of Jaffa.

In a journey filled with difficulty, this was the hardest part yet. It was extremely hot and dusty, with scorching sand blowing in all directions and obscuring any views out the train windows. The train itself jolted and jogged its way along the tracks, so it was impossible to sleep. Immigration procedures at the border took several hours. Everyone, Golda included, was exhausted from the weeks of difficult, nonstop travel. Much later, Golda confessed to wondering whether she would ever reach Palestine.

Still, Golda kept her group's spirits buoyed, leading them in rousing song. Her excitement proved contagious. After all, she told her companions, they were on the verge of arriving in Palestine! It would be a matter of hours before they were working the land!

On July 14, 1921, disembarking at the train station in Tel Aviv, Golda got her first glimpse of the promised land. It was a bleaker sight than she had imagined. Poverty was rampant. Beggars, covered with flies, moved through the crowds, beseeching travelers for handouts. Disease, especially malaria, plagued both the Arab and Jewish populations. It was also very, very hot.

There was "sand, blazing sand — that was all," she later wrote. After all the stories of pioneers "making the desert bloom," it was a complete and utter disappointment. Golda didn't laugh when one of the new arrivals said to her, half in jest, "Well, Goldie, you wanted to come to . . . Israel. Here we are. Now we can all go back." But Golda had come to Palestine to work the land, and she intended to do so. For new immigrants in the 1920s, this meant joining a *kibbutz*.

A kibbutz is a communal, or collective, settlement in which the welfare of the community is the number-one concern and individual needs or desires are secondary. It represents the practical application of the Labor Zionist ideal of social justice. In fact, some people dreamed that the state of Israel would be one large kibbutz!

The first kibbutz was founded at Degania, near the Sea of Galilee, by a group of pioneers working for the Palestine Land Development Company. Eventually, inspired by the teachings of A.D. Gordon and others, they overtook responsibility for the running of the farm. Other groups followed suit in many parts of the country, and the kibbutz soon became one of the models for Jews resettling Palestine.

Generally speaking, in a kibbutz one main building serves as a combination dining hall, meeting hall, and theater. Living quarters are usually small. Children are raised in "children's houses," and sleep apart from their parents, although in recent years children's houses have been used less and less. Jobs — for instance, in the kibbutz's fields, factories, animal coops, dining hall, or business office — are rotated among "kibbutzniks" so that everyone contributes equally.

All kibbutzim — in Hebrew, adding *im* to the end of a word means there is more than one — are part of a larger kibbutz movement. Schooling, medical services, and the other basics are provided by kibbutz members or by individuals from other kibbutzim, depending on their qualifications.

It is a unique and challenging living arrangement — one that satisfied the needs of the Zionist movement in several ways. First, the Jews needed an efficient way to settle and farm land in Palestine. The kibbutz brought together teams of workers with common interests. Second, the Jews needed new outposts in remote areas of the country, especially on its borders. The kibbutz was an effective way to make this risky enterprise more appealing. Finally, working together on a kibbutz with other dedicated Zionists made the pioneers love the land, more than any song, pep rally, or speech ever could.

Golda was astonished to learn that she and her friends couldn't simply report to a kibbutz and set to work. Instead, "candidates" for "membership" were scrutinized very carefully as to their spirit and physical fitness. This meant that Golda and Morris had to spend the summer of 1921 in Tel Aviv, where housing and jobs were scarce.

After a few days of furious apartment-hunting, a small place was located. It had no electricity, and the bathroom and kitchen had to be shared with forty other people. Golda found work giving private English lessons, and Morris took a job as a bookkeeper for part of the British administration. They planned to submit formal applications to Kibbutz Merhavia in the fall, as required.

Golda was disappointed by the delay in getting onto a kibbutz. In addition, the difficult living conditions in Tel Aviv made her wonder if maybe the Lithuanians had been right. Maybe she wasn't cut out for the life in Palestine. But she remained optimistic. After all, she had made it this far, and was about to begin the fulfillment of something she had been working toward for years. As she wrote in a letter to Shamai in Chicago:

"The surprising thing . . . is that only the new immigrants who only recently arrived are talking about leaving the country, whereas the older workers are still full of excitement. In my opinion, as long as they are here, those who with their own hands created even this little bit, I must not leave the land and you must immigrate."

Golda and Morris had picked Kibbutz Merhavia because a friend from Milwaukee had gone there. At first, their application was denied. To the hard-working kibbutzniks, married couples were not ideal candidates. The kibbutz members assumed married couples would eventually want children. Children couldn't help out with work and would have to be taken care of by someone. This meant there would be one less hand to get other work done.

In addition, some members of Merhavia thought Golda was a "spoiled" American girl. Others noted her experience as a teacher and said she might prove to be an "intellectual," not cut out to be a pioneer. The Meyersons, disturbed at the resistance they encountered, asked if they could work on the kibbutz for a trial period, in which they could dispel any doubts about their suitability. The kibbutzniks agreed.

Merhavia was located ten miles south of the Arab city of Nazareth, in the valley of Jezre'el in Palestine's north. The settlement then consisted of a few frame houses, a shack which served as a communal kitchen and bakery, and some trees casting occasional shade. The rest, as elsewhere in Palestine, consisted of sun-scorched fields. Thirty-two men and eight women worked amid the heat, swarming mosquitoes, flies, and gnats.

Golda once described how they defended themselves against all the insects: "Our only defense was Vaseline — which we smeared on the exposed parts of our bodies and on to which the gnats and flies resolutely stuck." There was also the ever-present threat of Arab attack.

Golda and Morris were given the toughest jobs to perform. Morris cleared rocks from fields so that planting could be done. Golda worked in the kitchen and then in the chicken coops. It was the toughest trial of their young lives. And although the jobs were done to perfection, and with a smile, the kibbutz members met three times before approving the couple's admission.

Golda Meir hard at work on the Kibbutz Merhavia in Palestine. Although she loved the communal farm life, it was a constant struggle against heat, swarms of insects, and the ever-present threat of Arab attack. Soon, the young Jews had transformed the dry, treeless land into a garden.

Golda liked to joke that it wasn't their work but Morris's record collection and record player that finally secured their admission.

Whatever the case, Golda loved kibbutz life. "Imagine!" she wrote. "Just imagine living by our own labor in a community where we're all equal, no rich or poor, no snobbery, no exploitation! . . . I enjoyed everything about the kibbutz — whether it was working in the chicken coops, learning the mysteries of kneading dough for bread in the little shack we used as a bakery or sharing a midnight snack with the boys coming back from guard duty and staying on in the kitchen for hours to hear their stories. After a very short time I felt completely at home, as though I had never lived anywhere else."

Golda quickly made her presence known. Given the task of reorganizing the communal kitchen, her first innovation was to serve oatmeal for breakfast, much to the kibbutzniks' chagrin. Golda believed that a good, hearty meal was needed to start the day. Though the kibbutzniks considered oatmeal "baby food," it was all that they had.

She changed the rest of the kibbutz diet to avoid what everyone had been eating most of the time — chickpeas cooked in bitter oil. And she introduced some delicate, American touches such as tablecloths and wildflower bouquets on each table for the traditional Sabbath meal on Friday night. Golda later worked in the almond groves and in the chicken coops. She organized the chickens so well, her plan became a model for other kibbutzim to follow!

Golda was such an exemplary kibbutznik that it

wasn't long before she was chosen to represent Merhavia to other kibbutzim in Palestine. She began traveling and speaking at various events and meetings, much as she had for Poale Zion in the United States. She was made the kibbutz's delegate to the prestigious council of the *Histadrut*, the Jewish General Federation of Labor. In 1922, she was the Merhavia delegate to a kibbutz convention held at Degania. There she met many of the major personalities of the *Yishuv*, among them Levi Eshkol, who would someday become prime minister of Israel, Berl Katznelson, who was a leading Zionist intellectual, and David Ben-Gurion.

Ben-Gurion was a Russian-Polish Jew who had once boasted as a child that "One day I will be the leader of Israel." After arriving in Palestine in 1906, he made good on that claim. He worked as a farm laborer and, in addition to being one of the founders of the Histadrut in 1920, he helped found *Hashomer*, a Jewish defense organization, later renamed *Haganah*. His courageous activism, as well as the strength of his beliefs and wisdom, quickly made him the leader of the Yishuv.

Ben-Gurion's official position at the time was general secretary of the Histadrut. In name, the Histadrut was the General Federation of Hebrew Workers of the Land of Israel. But Ben-Gurion made the Histadrut one of the dominant forces in the Yishuv by involving it in construction, land ownership, education, social and cultural services. All of these enterprises were managed by the workers themselves.

The other main organizations serving the Jews of Palestine were the Jewish Agency and the World Zionist Organization. The latter, founded by Herzl in 1897, was

41

an international network of Zionist organizations based in London and led by Chaim Weizmann, who had assumed leadership of the Zionist movement after Herzl's death. The WZO's main functions were fund-raising and diplomacy outside the Yishuv. The Jewish Agency, meanwhile, was the political arm of the nationhood effort. It had been set up by the terms of the British in 1922 as a quasi- or "shadow" government for Jewish activity in Palestine. Ben-Gurion would become head of the Jewish Agency in 1935, and Golda, too, would became one of its leading figures.

But as Golda prospered at kibbutz life and Yishuv politics, Morris had come to thoroughly dislike kibbutz life, both physically and spiritually. He had contracted malaria, suffered a hernia from the strenuous work, and had a stomach in constant uproar from the unfamiliar diet. Intellectually, he abhorred the lack of privacy that was a primary characteristic of kibbutz life. He missed Golda, longed for a traditional domestic life with wife and children, and was determined not to raise a child in the kibbutz's children's house. His differences with Golda could not have been greater.

Morris had gone along with Golda's wish to emigrate to Palestine. This time, when Morris suggested they leave the kibbutz, it was Golda who compromised. Golda thought that moving "to town" might revive Morris's health and their marriage. Still, it was a sad step for her to take.

"For him I made the biggest sacrifice of my life: I left the kibbutz," she wrote. "You see, there was nothing I loved so much as the kibbutz. I liked everything about the kibbutz: the manual work, the comradeship, the

42

discomforts . . . . In the beginning it had nothing to offer but swamps and sand, but soon it became a garden full of orange trees, fruits, and just to look at it gave me such joy that I could have spent my whole life there."

In the end, for Golda the issue came down a very basic fact. Morris had followed her to Palestine to have a wife. She was obliged to follow him to Tel Aviv to start a family.

6

The Wretched Years

GOLDA ONCE DESCRIBED the period immediately following her time on a kibbutz as the "wretched" years. The couple's life in Tel Aviv consisted almost entirely of finding enough food to eat and trying to make ends meet. Golda worked as a cashier in the Office of Public Works of Histadrut — known as the Solel Boneh. Morris recuperated from the effects of his various kibbutz-inflicted maladies. He remained angry at Golda for his dilapidated physical condition. Golda remained angry at him for forcing her to leave the kibbutz life she loved so dearly.

Then, on the same day that Golda learned she was pregnant, she was offered a transfer to the Solel Boneh office in Jerusalem. A job for Morris, as a bookkeeper, was available as well. This seemed to be a good omen, and the couple readily made the move to Jerusalem and settled into a two-room apartment in a religious neighborhood.

Morris loved Jerusalem. Its book shops, and its spiritual climate — it is the holy city of Judaism, Islam, and Christianity — appealed to his interests and sensitivities. Golda, however, felt depressed at their continued poverty. Their new apartment had no gas and no electricity, and they were forced to take in a boarder to help with the rent. At times, she was reminded of the stories her mother told of the impoverished Mabovitch household in the Pale of Settlement.

The joy of the birth of a little baby boy, whom they named Menachem, in November 1924 did little to alter Golda's feelings of loneliness and aimlessness. She was twenty-six years old and, she reminded herself, had come to Palestine to help build a country. The life she was now living, she later wrote, had "little meaning." In May 1925, Golda took Menachem and returned to Merhavia. Though Golda returned to Jerusalem just six months later, her marriage to Morris had begun its long and painful slide toward a permanent separation.

The couple's second child, Sarah, was born the following year. With no room left for a boarder, the couple were going to have problems paying their bills. Golda worked as a laundress at Menachem's nursery school in exchange for tuition there, and then taught English in a private school. Since she couldn't afford a babysitter, she took the kids along with her to this job.

Golda felt like a prisoner, and told friends she wanted to return to work — that is, to work for the Zionist movement. She was determined to become involved in the affairs of her people, no matter what it meant. This, she decided, was her calling. It didn't take long for Golda to find a place in the movement. In 1928 she was made secretary of the Women's Labor Council

(WLC), a part of the Histadrut, and its representative at the executive committee of the Histadrut. The job meant a move back to Tel Aviv and a good deal of overseas travel, mostly to England and the United States.

Golda threw herself wholeheartedly into the job, developing "working women's farms," day-care facilities, and kindergartens. She traveled all the time, and would for the next six years.

Morris understood that this was yet another blow to their marriage. He had moved out of the family home, and moved back in again, reflecting the changing fortunes of their off-and-on relationship.

Golda held out hope that her happiness at work might translate into a better marriage and family life for everyone. Her days were filled with an impossible array of tasks — cooking, cleaning, shopping, meetings, and the like — that had her moving about in a veritable frenzy. She tried to compensate for her long absences from home and the children by lavishing them with gifts from abroad and extra attention when she was home. She was not always successful.

"I know that my children, when they were little, suffered a lot on my account. I left them alone so often . . . . Oh, I remember how happy they were, my children, every time I didn't go to work because of a headache. They jumped and laughed and sang, 'Mamma's staying home! Mamma has a headache!' And still . . . still I have to be honest and ask myself, Golda, deep in your heart do you really regret the fact that you behaved as you did with them? No."

Golda's deepening commitment to the Zionist movement came at a time of increasing turmoil, both in Pales-

47

tine and in Europe. The movement had made significant gains throughout the 1920s. Jewish immigrants continued to flow into Palestine. The cities of Tel Aviv and Haifa, and kibbutzim throughout the country, grew. And the movement's major organizations — the Jewish Agency, the World Zionist Organization, and the Histadrut — solidified their standing.

But in 1929 the Arabs staged a summer-long uprising that took the lives of more than one hundred Jews and destroyed huge amounts of property. Many Jews likened the attacks to those they had experienced in the Pale of Settlement. In response, the British restricted Jewish immigration and land purchases, striking at the very heart of Zionist activities.

Meanwhile, in Germany, an extremist politician was gaining widespread support for his plan to end what he called the "Jewish problem." His name was Adolf Hitler, and he was the leader of the Nazi Party.

Against this backdrop, Golda's work couldn't help but have the impact she desired. In 1928-1929, she served as the WLC's delegate to its American Zionist counterpart, the Pioneer Women's Organization. The PWO made substantial contributions to the Zionist movement, and it was Golda's task to report to the women, most of whom not been to Palestine, and to maintain their support. In America, Golda also visited her sister Clara, whom she had not seen for many years. Clara was married and had a son.

In 1932, Golda's daughter Sarah fell so ill with a kidney disease that doctors in Palestine recommended treatment in the United States. In fact, they were concerned about Sarah's ability to even survive the trip!

Golda asked to be sent to the United States as the national secretary of the PWO, and brought Sarah and Menachem with her. Morris moved to Haifa.

It was quickly discovered that Sarah was indeed ill with kidney disease — but not the one that had been diagnosed in Palestine. She recovered within six weeks. Golda stayed in America for two years, crisscrossing the country many times, speaking about developments in Palestine. She developed a special relationship with American Jews.

It was during the early 1930s that Golda had another encounter with David Ben-Gurion, the leader of the Yishuv. Having attended a speech of hers in London, he wrote to the Jewish newspaper *Ha'aretz*: "She spoke with genius, assertively, bitterly, with hurt, and sensibly. Although I had heard of her success in the women's convention and other gatherings arranged for her by the labor movement in different places, her speech was a great surprise to me."

Indeed, Golda had risen to such prominence within the movement in the past six years that, upon her return to Palestine in 1934, she was offered a more challenging position — a place on *Vaad Hapoel*, the Histadrut's executive committee. The executive committee was the unofficial cabinet of the Yishuv government. Her colleagues included Ben-Gurion, Moshe Sharett, Zalman Shazar, and a number of other prominent Zionists.

Golda's first assignment in this new post was to direct the department of tourism, which meant conducting tours for visiting officials and dignitaries from other countries, whose help was being cultivated for the Zionist movement.

49

Her ascent in Zionist politics continued in 1935, when she became a member of Vaad Hapoel's steering committee, or secretariat. She was eventually put in charge of the Trade Union and Labor Relations Council, and of the Workers' Sick Fund, which served more than 100,000 people. Both positions put her into direct contact with the day-to-day difficulties of people throughout the Yishuv. And because she often had to champion some unpopular causes in the face of strong opposition, it was here that she came into her own as a forthright, earnest, and humane leader.

One of the features of the Yishuv economy was a fixed wage scale. This meant that every worker started with the same fixed wage, and that any increase in that wage came only with seniority or an increase in the number of dependents. In other words, a worker with nine children would earn more than one with two. Likewise, professionals such as lawyers and doctors earned the same as truckers and janitors, despite their protests that their jobs were more valuable and therefore merited more pay.

Golda resisted many workers' demands to change the system, believing it to be fair. Likewise, Golda stood her ground on the need for an unemployment fund. This angered much of Palestine's work force, since the funds for unemployment payments had to come from payments made into it by workers. That "donation" amounted to the equivalent of a day's pay per month, a lot of money in a time of hardship.

Golda was pleased to campaign on behalf of the project known as *Nachshon*, for it meant jobs for Histadrut workers and an overall improvement in the Jewish economic potential. Nachshon, Hebrew for the first of the Israelites to jump into the parted waters of the Red Sea during the Exodus from Egypt, was to be the Histadrut's shipping enterprise. Golda traveled to the United States to solicit funds for the project, and a port of Tel Aviv was constructed.

The rationale behind Nachshon was threefold. The Jews would no longer have to rely on the Arab port of Jaffa. The Jews would be "returning" to the sea, as they had already returned to the land. Golda herself confessed that part of the project's appeal was the romantic ideal of Jewish sailors and Jewish seamen plying waters from Europe to Asia and Africa.

But there was another pragmatic aspect to Nachshon: increasing tumult and discrimination in Europe meant that the Jews there might need to escape. The sea was their only route, and the Yishuv wanted to be ready for them. In fact, such immigration was fast becoming a matter of life and death for many European Jews.

By the early 1930s, Hitler had become the dictator of Germany. He had portrayed himself as a powerful leader devoted to the German "fatherland." This image had great appeal because of severe economic difficulties and because of the awful memories many Germans had of their country's terrible defeat in World War I. To the rest of Europe, however, and to much of the civilized world in general, Hitler was a threat to the peace.

Hitler also championed racist ideas, declaring the Germans to be a "pure" race destined to rule the world. He singled out the Jews as a "cancer" who had "soiled" Germany and were responsible for all of society's ills. They should be destroyed, he maintained, and sought to do so, first through harassment and humiliation, then through more excessive forms of discrimination. Jews were denied jobs, housing, and education, and were beaten, boycotted, and forced to live in ghettos. Such practices became the law in Germany by 1935.

The appalling beliefs of Hitler and his Nazi government led to a dramatic rise in the number of Jews in Palestine. By 1939 some 450,000 had entered the country. The local Arabs were not pleased, and began calling for an Arab state in Palestine. Other Arab states in the region — Syria, Transjordan, and Iraq — had already been granted independence or autonomy by the colonial powers of France and Britain. The Palestinian Arabs wanted the same for themselves. The competition over tiny Palestine grew more and more fierce.

In April 1936, after months of tension, the Arabs staged an organized uprising known as the Arab Revolt. Britain ferried in extra troops from Egypt, Malta, and England in an attempt to restore order. The British government also appointed a commission to investigate the situation and make recommendations.

In June 1937, the Peel Commission, named for the man who headed it, Lord William Robert Wellesley Peel, proposed a novel, startling solution that no one had ever considered. He suggested dividing the disputed territories into two separate, independent states. This controversial idea became known as "partition."

Yishuv leaders were split over the idea. On the one hand, they said, Britain seemed to be thinking in terms of an actual state for the Jews. This was definitely more than vague words about a Jewish "homeland." However, others found it difficult to conceive of a Jewish state smaller than the borders it had in biblical times.

Golda felt that the Jews would be giving up too much if they agreed to partition Palestine. The Jewish state, she said, would be too small and crowded to be viable. Eventually, though, Golda came to agree with the majority, which also included Ben-Gurion and Chaim Weizmann. Their position could be summed up very easily — that half a loaf is better than none.

Developments in Europe again took center stage. The German Army had occupied Austria and parts of Czechoslovakia in 1938. On September 29, English Prime Minister Chamberlain signed the Munich Pact with Adolf Hitler. The Munich Pact was supposed to put a stop to German aggression, by allowing Hitler's soldiers to stay in parts of Czechoslovakia. However, statesmen everywhere believed that Germany would not honor the agreement. Indeed, historians now say that the Munich Pact contributed to the outbreak of another world war. Jews in Palestine worried that the British might also give in to Arab demands, just as they had given in to Hitler.

Less than six weeks later, on November 8, Britain fed those fears with the release of a report stating that partition of Palestine could not work. The commission that had prepared the report — dubbed the "Re-Peel Commission" by some cynical Zionists — offered a "best-case" scenario: a Jewish state of some 400 square miles along Palestine's coastal plain.

That night, as the Jews reeled from this blow, German Jews suffered through something far worse. In a night of rampage and wanton violence, Hitler's storm troopers sacked and burned homes, synagogues, and shops owned by Jews. They beat and arrested vast numbers of Jewish people. The event came to be known as Kristallnacht or "Crystal Night" because of the shattered glass strewn throughout the Jewish neighborhoods of Germany. Kristallnacht also marked the beginning of what Hitler called his "final solution" to the "Jewish problem."

The situation was discussed at the International Conference on Refugees, called by U.S. President Franklin Delano Roosevelt and held in the summer of 1939 in Evian-les-Bains, France. The conference was attended by leaders and delegates from thirty-two countries. Golda was there as the "observer" from Palestine. Having no official voice, she was seated not among the delegates but in the audience, even though the refugees under discussion were, as she put it, "her family."

One by one the leaders rose to express their sympathy for the plight of refugees — the poor, persecuted Jews. And one by one they explained why they could not open the doors of their countries. There were quotas, they said, as well as huge problems in accepting large numbers of foreign people. Golda felt a mixture of sorrow, rage, frustration, and horror. As she wrote in her autobiography, "I wanted to get up and scream at them all, 'Don't you know that these "numbers" are human beings, people who may spend the rest of their lives in concentration camps . . . ?' "

Golda tried behind-the-scenes lobbying to get some of the representatives to change their minds, but to no avail. In effect, the conference had been one big failure for the persecuted Jews. Golda called a press conference to speak her mind before going home. Her stinging comments to the assembled crowd of reporters and photographers were broadcast for all to hear. "There is only one thing I hope to see before I die, and that is that my people should not need expressions of sympathy any more."

As the outbreak of war looked more and more certain, the British began to fear that the Arabs would switch sides and support the Germans to achieve their aims in Palestine. They remembered that the Arabs had fought with them during World War I, when the goal was to oust the Turks from the region. The Arabs also controlled enormous reserves of oil, as well as military outposts along the Suez Canal, which were always important in peacetime but would be absolutely vital for the war effort.

In an attempt to win the Arabs' support, Great Britain hardened its policy toward the Jews in Palestine. In May 1939 the British government issued another "White Paper." It stipulated that Jewish immigration to Palestine would end following the admission of 75,000 immigrants over the next five years.

This meant that the Jews would forever be a minority in Palestine. The White Paper also limited the amount of Arab land Jews could buy, and said that British policy did not back the establishment of a Jewish state in Palestine. The Zionists were outraged. A livid Chaim Weizmann called the White Paper a "death sentence."

In August 1939, Golda Meyerson journeyed to Geneva, Switzerland, for what was to be the last Zionist Congress before the war. The main topic of debate was the thorny dilemma faced by the Yishuv. Britain, an ally in the fight against Hitler, was also now an enemy in the struggle for a Jewish state. Which was more important?

Golda and the others decided to continue immigration, settlement activity, and self-defense efforts, believing it to be their right as Jews. These activities would continue, they declared, even if it came to armed clashes against the British. As Ben-Gurion put it, "We shall fight Hitler as if there were no White Paper, and fight the White Paper as if there were no Hitler."

While the Zionist Congress was in session, the Soviet Union and Germany announced that they had reached a non-aggression pact. This was cause for alarm. Everyone knew that both of those countries had territorial ambitions in Poland. It meant that war was going to happen sooner rather than later. Sure enough, on September 1, the Germans invaded Poland, and Nazi bombs rained down on Warsaw, the capital. Two days later France and Great Britain declared war on Germany. World War II had begun.

Golda returned to Palestine. The other delegates to the Congress went back to their homes. Most of them would not survive the war. No one knew what would happen next. Jewish relations with Britain were strained. Their lives in Europe were threatened. They were not welcome in Palestine, their purported homeland. It seemed as if the Zionist movement had come to the end of the road.

56

7

A State Is Born

FOR THE JEWS of Europe, the Second World War meant genocide — the murder of an entire race of people. As the German armies spread throughout the continent, Jews were shipped to death camps. Most were killed immediately, while others were used as slaves and either worked to death or murdered. In the next six years, millions of Jews perished in the camps. Their bodies were cremated — but only after the Nazis had taken their jewelry and gold teeth, and stuffed mattresses with their hair and used their body fat to make soap.

"I have sometimes wondered how we got through those years without going to pieces," Golda wrote of the war. Among the most agonizing things she faced was the sight of the British fighting valiantly against the Nazis, while simultaneously turning their backs on the very victims of those Nazis. It was British policy in Palestine, almost as much as World War II itself, that turned the struggle for a Jewish state into a matter of utmost urgency.

During the war, Golda served on Britain's War Economic Advisory Council as a liaison between the British authorities in Palestine and the public. She continued to work to improve the conditions of the Yishuv economy and its workers. And like many of her fellow Zionists, she became a member of the Haganah, the underground Jewish defense force.

Following a general policy of *havlagah*, or restraint, the Haganah was a defensive force, to be used only if Jews or their property were attacked. Weizmann and Ben-Gurion, shepherding the Yishuv through this difficult time, did not want to antagonize the Arabs or jeopardize innocent lives.

One of the Haganah's major wartime initiatives was the attempt to smuggle immigrants into Palestine by boat. These were Jews who had managed, somehow, to escape Nazi-controlled territory in the hope of gaining passage to Palestine. But the British refused entry to Palestine to these refugees. Ships that reached the shores of Palestine were often turned away, their desperate human cargo sent back where they had come from, or placed in internment camps on the island of Cyprus, south of Turkey.

Some of the would-be immigrants were expelled even after they had set foot on land and kissed the beach out of sheer joy at their arrival. In November 1940, Jews aboard the S.S. *Patria* blew up their ship rather than obey with an order by the British to sail for the island of Mauritius in the Indian Ocean. More than 250 men, women, and children drowned as a result. Another ship, the S.S. *Struma*, sank off the coast of Istanbul in February 1942 after months in immigration limbo.

Seven hundred and sixty-nine people — the ship normally carried one hundred — lost their lives.

The British clamped down on the Jews in Palestine proper as well. In September 1943, Golda was called to testify at the trial of two young Palestinian Jews. They were accused of having volunteered for the British Army so they could steal arms for the Haganah. Sworn by oath to tell the truth about what she knew, Golda also had to be careful not to reveal any Haganah secrets.

The British prosecutor was trying to establish that the Jewish Agency, a legal organization, was working hand in hand with the Haganah, an illegal one. He also wanted to make it look as if the Haganah was not a self-defense organization but a band of terrorists. Golda would need to walk a tightrope with her testimony.

The prosecutor began his questioning with a simple question, posed in a slightly sarcastic tone.

"You are a nice, peaceful, law-abiding lady, are you not?"

"I think I am," Golda responded, with equal sarcasm.

"And you have always been so?"

"I have never been accused of anything," she replied.

The courtroom came astir. Golda had taken a defiant tone with the British, something they were certain not to like. The prosecutor went on.

"Have you trained the Jewish youth in the use of fire-arms?"

"Jewish youth will defend Jewish life and property in the events of riots and the necessity to defend life and property. I, as well as other Jews, would defend myself."

"Have you heard of 'Haganah'?"

"Yes."

"Do they have arms?"

"I don't know, but I suppose they have."

And so it continued, the prosecutor probing, and Golda not revealing any more than she had to. People watching the trial were impressed with Golda's fortitude. She was even bold enough to use the witness box as her podium. At one point she stated proudly, "If a Jew who is armed in self-defense is a criminal, then all the Jews in Palestine are criminals."

Golda's answers were not much different than they would have been in a friend's living room or at a Zionist gathering. But her performance earned her the respect of many of her Yishuv colleagues. Some historians have said the event marked the beginning of Golda's political career.

World War II ended with the unconditional surrender of Germany in May 1945 and of Japan in August, after two Japanese cities were devastated by atomic bombs. It was a time of rejoicing, but of sad reckoning as well. Six million Jews, one third of the entire Jewish population in the world, had died in what has come to be called the Holocaust. The remaining Jews seemed no nearer a state than before the war. For Golda, the lesson of the Holocaust was clear. Jews needed sovereignty. As she wrote, "If there had been a tiny state during the days of the Holocaust, we would have saved many Jews."

After the war, many Zionists in Palestine thought the British would finally allow the tattered remains of European Jewry into the country, and perhaps even re-think their policy toward the Jewish homeland. They were wrong. U.S. President Harry Truman made statements of support for the formation of a Jewish state, saying that 100,000 refugees from Germany and Austria should be allowed in as a simple humanitarian gesture. But the British didn't agree.

When an "Anglo American Committee of Inquiry" was formed to look into the issue, Golda testified at hearings held in Palestine in March 1946. "We Jews," she told the commission, "only want that which is given naturally to all the peoples of the world, to be masters of our own fate." The commission recommended, like Truman, that 100,000 Jews be allowed to enter. But the British spurned the committee's work and ignored its counsel.

These developments were particular maddening for socialist Jews such as Golda. They had put their faith in the new British Labor Government that had come to power in July 1945, promising to rescind the White Paper and work for the creation of a Jewish state in Palestine. The Zionists had celebrated when Labor triumphed, thinking the election marked "a clear victory for the demands of Zionism." It took hardly any time at all for the cheers to turn to cries of outrage.

First, the British set a monthly immigration quota of 1,500 at a time when thousands of refugees could have poured in daily. Second, foreign secretary Ernest Bevin displayed a remarkable insensitivity to the meaning of the Holocaust by saying that the Jewish survivors still had a future in Europe. Ben-Gurion voiced the fury of the entire Yishuv when he said, "The acts of the British government are a continuation of Hitler's policy of hos-

61

tility." The Yishuv vowed to continue its efforts at smuggling in refugees.

In April 1946, the British captured two ships, the *Fede* and the *Eliahu Golomb*, each carrying over 1,000 refugees, in the Mediterranean Sea off the coast of Italy. Instead of turning themselves over to the British, the refugees called a hunger strike, vowing to eat only when the ships were allowed to set sail for Palestine. The Zionists had discovered a new weapon to use against the British — international publicity.

Golda suggested that some of the Yishuv's leaders join the strike, to draw further attention to the ships' plight. Though Golda had recently been released from the hospital after a gall bladder attack, she chose to participate.

Golda and twelve other leaders set themselves up in a courtyard of the Vaad Leumi — the elected National Council — offices. Sympathetic friends and well-wishers dropped by to offer encouragement, sing songs, pray, or simply be part of the occasion. The fasters drank tea but ate no solid food. The third day of the fast was Passover, the holiday commemorating the Jews' flight from bondage in Egypt. Golda and the others ate a small, ceremonial piece of matzoh, the unleavened bread made on Passover.

On the fourth day of the hunger strike, the already starved, frail, and crowded refugees gave in to hunger and gave up their strike. However, they announced that for each day their ship was held up, ten men and ten women would kill themselves. The threat worked. On May 8, the British allowed the ships to sail. Golda and the others ended their fast after 104 hours.

These actions had gained the Zionists favorable worldwide publicity. But the two ships were almost the only ones able to reach Palestine in the years after the war. Between 1945 and 1948, of the sixty-three ships loaded with Jewish refugees that set sail for Palestine, only five got through.

Most of Golda's time was spent on the problem of refugees. The "displaced person" (D.P.) camps — places where refugees from the war were kept in countries outside of Palestine — were miserably crowded places. The rate of infant mortality was especially high, and it was a problem Golda thought deserved to be at the top of her list.

Normally, people who waited the longest in the camps had the first opportunity to go to Palestine. Golda convinced the British to agree to a change in the "first in, first out" policy so that families with children and infants would be allowed to leave first. To put this agreement into action, she had to convince the refugees themselves that this was a sound plan — even though some people who had just arrived would, because they had a baby, be able to depart for Palestine before others who had been in the camps for months. There was only one way for Golda to do this — by going to the camps and speaking directly with the people there.

The camps were indeed like prison camps. Cities of crude huts and tents, there was not enough water for drinking and bathing. Though the camps were located on the shore, no swimming was allowed. Internees spent their time in their stifling tents, awaiting news of their fate. Golda spoke candidly and managed to convince many of them to give up their rightful spots on the

immigration lists in favor of the children. She returned
to Palestine deeply disturbed by what she had seen, and
convinced — not that she needed convincing — of the
urgency of her cause.

Eventually Jewish opposition to the British took on
a more militant character. Two dissident Jewish military groups were formed, the *Irgun Z'vai Leumi* (National Military Organization), and *Lohamei Herut Israel*
or Lehi (Fighters for Freedom of Israel), known to English speakers as the Stern Gang after Avraham Stern,
the group's founder. These organizations disagreed
with the Haganah's defensive nature, that Jews should
fight back only when threatened and attacked. They believed that an aggressive approach to the British and
the Arabs would secure Jewish sovereignty.

The Irgun and Lehi attacked railway installations
and British police targets, raided British arms depots,
destroyed planes belonging to the Royal Air Force, and
blew up the bridges connecting Palestine to neighboring
Arab countries.

On June 29, 1946, the British responded with a mas-
sive operation against the Yishuv. On a day that came
to be known as Black Saturday, nearly 3,000 Jews were
detained, among them some of the movement's leaders,
and a curfew was put in place. British soldiers swooped
down upon Tel Aviv and searched, block by block,
house by house, for arms and for resistance fighters in
hiding. Ben-Gurion was in Paris at the time, and he
knew he would be arrested if he returned to Palestine.
When the British had finished seizing most of the Zionist leaders, Golda, the head of the political department

of the Jewish Agency, was the leading spokesperson for the Yishuv in Palestine.

But less than a month later, before she had had any time to bring some calm to a tense country, the Irgun blew up the British headquarters in Palestine, the King David Hotel in Jerusalem. Twenty-eight Britons, fourty-one Arabs, seventeen Jews, two Armenians, one Russian, one Greek, and one Egyptian were killed in an attack that has been called a "tragedy of errors" and remains one of the most controversial incidents in Israel's history. The Haganah itself denounced the Irgun. Still, the bombing did cause the British to begin asking themselves whether their presence in Palestine was worth the trouble.

The situation then went from bad to worse. Violence continued between Arabs and Jews, and by extremist Jews against the British. Finally, in the spring of 1947, Britain pronounced the situation in Palestine "unworkable." The British government sought the help of the United Nations to work out a solution. Britain also said that it would withdraw from Palestine on May 15, 1948, no matter what. The long-awaited end of British rule was at hand. But who would govern Palestine when the British were gone?

Many attempts were made to answer this question. At the United Nations in New York, delegates from all the countries in the world decided to vote on "partition" — dividing Palestine into two independent countries, one for Jews and one for Arabs.

Among the most intriguing and astonishing were secret negotiations conducted between the Jews and the man regarded as the local leader most willing to live in peace with the Jews — King Abdullah of Transjordan, a country that is now called Jordan. Golda was chosen to represent the Jews.

On November 17, 1947, accompanied by two Israeli experts on Arabs, she met with Abdullah in a house in the town of Naharayim, near a bridge that joined Palestine with Transjordan. After getting over his initial surprise at seeing that a woman headed the Jewish delegation, Abdullah explained to his guests that the quarrel was really not between the Jews and the Arabs. The quarrel, he said, was between the Arabs and the British and between the Jews and the British.

The King went on to propose that the Jews agree to a Hebrew Republic within Transjordan, with Abdullah as sovereign of this "federation." Golda reminded the King that the United Nations' partition plan offered a solution based on two independent states, not one, a better deal than the King seemed to be offering.

The talks ended without a solution, but both sides promised to meet again after the vote in the United Nations. Golda came away from the encounter thinking that, unlike other Arab leaders, the King had peaceful intentions.

Less than two weeks later, the UN General Assembly was going to meet in New York to vote on the partition plan. Though there were some dissenters, and even some reluctance on the part of those who supported the idea, the Zionists were in favor of the partition plan. They preferred to have a partitioned homeland rather than continued uncertainty and violence. They hoped enough nations would agree. A two-thirds majority of all votes cast was required for passage. If everyone was present and voted, thirty-eight out of the fifty-seven member nations in the UN would have to vote "yes" for the Jewish dream to be realized.

The Jews were by no means assured passage. Theirs was but one issue on a complicated and busy international agenda. And what would tiny Israel have to offer in exchange for partition? A state of Israel would not be a superpower able to win friends with foreign aid and the latest technology. But the idea of Israel — a democratic country dedicated to the ideals of freedom and justice — and the drama of the country's rebirth after thousands of years, that was something the delegates could understand and react to!

Chaim Weizmann journeyed to the United States in October for what one historian called "one of the most intricate and dramatic lobbying exercises in modern diplomatic history." He addressed the UN, spoke with the delegates, and met with U.S. President Harry Truman. Still, as the day of the vote neared, Weizmann realized the Jews did not have enough votes. Jewish delegates managed to get the vote postponed for three days — and in this time the cajoling and persuading continued.

Finally, on November 29, 1947, at 5:35 P.M., time for the vote was at hand. Around the world, Jews gathered at their radios to listen to the broadcast of the vote. In Israel, people flocked to public squares in towns and villages, since the proceedings were broadcast over loudspeakers. Still other Jews prayed at the sacred site of the Wailing Wall in Jerusalem.

It took just three minutes for the delegates to reach their final tally: thirty-three for, thirteen against, ten abstentions, one absence. Since eleven delegates didn't vote, the plan needed only thirty-one votes, two-thirds of the forty-six who voted. The partition plan had passed by a margin of just two votes. The Zionist dream had come true!

It was past midnight in Palestine when the vote was taken, but 25,000 people packed the main square of Tel Aviv, erupting into song and dance. But Palestine's Jewish leaders knew that hard days were sure to follow. "The decision imposes heavy responsiblity on the Yishuv, and on the entire Jewish people," said Ben-Gurion.

Golda, listening at home, rushed to her office at the Jewish Agency in Jerusalem. There she found crowds dancing and singing in celebration. She immediately went out to the balcony of her office and spoke to the crowd.

"For two thousand years we have worked for our deliverance. Now that it is here, it is so great and wonderful that it surpasses words." She added a special appeal to the Palestinian Arabs: "Let us now live in friendship and peace together." Golda sensed that these last words might not have much effect. The Arabs, she knew, intended to fight. If they did, the Jews would have to fight back.

The Arabs objected to the partition plan for several reasons. First and foremost, they believed that Palestine was theirs, and had been for centuries. They asked why the Jews were being given a country in the Middle East as a solution to what had been a European problem. They thought the plan represented an effort by several strong countries to take advantage of a much weaker people. And they resented the colonialist, imperialist thinking that allowed major powers such as Britain, France, and the United States to have their way in the Middle East when it was really Arab territory. They vowed to come together in an effort to drive the Jews out of Palestine.

Arab assaults began quickly after the partition vote. With the May deadline less than six months away, the two sides began to prepare for war. While Golda's colleagues in the Yishuv made the physical preparations — training soldiers, for example — she realized that she was the one to raise the money the new state would need. As she told Ben-Gurion, "What you are doing here, I cannot do. However, what you propose to do in the United States, I can do."

Following her miraculous fund-raising success in the United States, Golda returned to Israel where she was instructed to meet again with King Abdullah of Transjordan. It was early May 1948, and the Jews hoped that the King would promise not to attack after the British pull-out, scheduled for one week later. This time, however, Abdullah refused to come to Naharayim. If Golda wanted to speak with him, she would have to make the perilous journey all the way to Amman, the Jordanian capital. Through his messengers, the King let it be known that he could not risk being discovered in talks with the enemy on the eve of war.

Golda assessed the risks and decided to go through with the mission. Donning black robes and a veil, she climbed into a car and sat in the back seat next to a man who pretended to be her "husband." His name was Ezra Danin. He was to serve as an interpreter, and was also dressed in Arab robes. The circuitous trip to Amman took three hours. The couple switched cars several times to make sure they weren't being followed. They made their way through various checkpoints without being discovered. Only when they got close to the king's palace were they assisted by one of Abdullah's emissaries.

The King wasted no time in getting right to the point. "Why are you in such a hurry to proclaim your state?" he demanded.

Golda knew how long she had waited, and how long the Jews had waited. She replied that 2,000 years should not be termed "a hurry." The King seemed to agree with this reasoning.

The conversation quickly reached a dead end, for Golda and the Zionists could not settle for vague promises of rights within an Arab-led entity, not after half a century of work and struggle for a state. Abdullah was committed to the united Arab front, which meant that he would be waging war, along with Syria, Iraq, Egypt, and Lebanon, to keep the Jewish state from coming into being. There was nothing left to say. The hope was expressed that talks could continue after the war.

On the way back to Palestine, Golda's driver refused to accompany her and Danin all the way to Naharayim. They would have to walk the rest of the way, undetected, through unfamiliar terrain. As Golda described the dangerous journey: "We didn't even dare to breathe too loudly. I was badly hampered by the clothes I was wearing, not at all sure that we were going in the right direction, and unable to shake off my depression and sense of failure about the talk with Abdullah." Eventually, they met up with a Haganah scout who guided them back to safety.

Several days later on May 14, Golda made her way to the Tel Aviv Art Museum for a special ceremony — the one at which the existence of the State of Israel would be proclaimed. Golda was fortunate to be in Tel Aviv for the momentous occasion. She had been ordered to Jerusalem, but mechanical trouble had forced her plane to turn back in mid-flight.

At four o'clock in the afternoon, Ben-Gurion rapped a gavel to bring the meeting to order and began to speak. He was cut off, however, by the sound of the two-hundred-strong crowd, which had spontaneously begun singing *Hatikvah* — "The Hope" — the new state's national anthem. Standing in front of a large picture of Theodor Herzl, Ben-Gurion continued to speak when the music stopped:

"The Land of Israel was the birthplace of the Jewish people. Here their spiritual, religious, and national identity was formed. Here they achieved independence and created a culture of national and universal significance. Here they wrote and gave the Bible to the world. Exiled from the Land of Israel the Jewish people remained faithful to it in all the centuries of their dispersion, never ceasing to pray and hope for their return and the restoration of their national freedom . . . . Accordingly, we, the members of the National Council, representing the Jewish people in the Land of Israel and the Zionist movement, have assembled on the day of the termination of the British Mandate for Palestine, and, by virtue of our natural and historic right and of the resolution of the General Assembly of the United Nations, do

71

hereby proclaim the establishment of a Jewish state in the land of Israel — the State of Israel."

Golda wept tears of joy. When her turn came to sign Israel's Declaration of Independence, she was crying so hard that someone had to assist her and guide her hand to the proper spot.

"After I signed, I cried," she said. "When I studied American history as a schoolgirl, and I read about those who signed the Declaration of Independence, I couldn't imagine these were real people doing something real. And there I was sitting down and signing a Declaration of Independence."

The hope, the fear, the longing, the accomplishment. All of these feelings came together that afternoon in Tel Aviv. Golda experienced them to their fullest, for she knew that they were but fleeting. The next day the war of survival began.

Golda Meir signing the Israeli Declaration of Independence in May 1948. She was so overjoyed she began to cry, and someone had to guide her hand to the proper spot. The next day, the neighboring countries declared war on the Jewish state, and Israel fought to survive.

8

Ambassador and Labor Minister

THE SPIRITED EMBRACES and congratulations of the museum gathering quickly gave way to the grim reality of war. The armies of five Arab states, aided by contingents from Saudi Arabia, Sudan, and Yemen, attacked Israel almost immediately. The fighting raged on until an armistice agreement was signed in early 1949. Israel was victorious, capturing the Negev Desert and most of the Upper and Lower Galilee regions — more territory than had been allotted to Israel in the partition agreement. But Syria controlled the Golan Heights overlooking the Hula Valley in Israel's north, and used this perch to rain gunfire down upon Israeli settlements below. Jordan had held onto Judea and Samaria, the biblical names for the regions on the West Bank of the Jordan River. As well, the eastern half of the city of Jerusalem, including the famed Old City and its religious sites, remained in Jordan. Although a "no-man's land" of mines and barbed wire divided the city, Israelis thought that peace would

75

come once the Arabs grew accustomed to the fact of a Jewish state in the Middle East.

Golda, still officially the head of the Jewish Agency's political department, spent the early days of the war in the United States on another fund-raising mission. The United Jewish Appeal had cabled Golda, telling her that she could raise *another* $50 million in the post-independence euphoria. Golda knew how much this would mean to the new state, and took the first plane bound for New York.

She was greeted by cheering crowds and found generous support wherever she went. "I spoke in city after city," she later recalled. "At lunches, dinners and teas and at parlor meetings in people's homes. Whenever I felt overwhelmed by fatigue — which was often — all I had to do was to remind myself that I was now talking as an emissary of a Jewish state, and my tiredness simply drained away."

But as much as Golda knew she was doing the right thing, she desperately wanted to be with her countrymen in the early days of Israel's existence. The distance was made all the more distressing when Golda learned of the loss of east Jerusalem. Across the centuries and throughout the Diaspora, longing for the city had come to symbolize the Jews' yearning for liberty and dignity. "Next year in Jerusalem" they had prayed each year at Passover for centuries. With the latest news, it appeared, they would be making this prayer for years yet to come.

Then another piece of upsetting news reached her. Moshe Sharett, foreign minister in a new government headed by Ben-Gurion, told her that she had been named Israel's first ambassador to the Soviet Union.

The world's greatest power after the United States had been one of the first nations to extend diplomatic recognition to the new state of Israel. Because Russia had a large Jewish population, it was especially important for Israel to cultivate good relations.

Golda was distressed at her new job. She had no pleasant memories of her life in the Soviet Union. Moscow was thousands of miles from Israel, her family, and her friends. To be sent so far away while historic events were unfolding in Israel seemed almost like exile. Still, she knew, her duty was to Israel, now more than ever.

In September 1948, Golda arrived in the Soviet capital. "If only the tsar could have seen that!" she crowed — gazing up at the Israeli flag flying from the top of the Hotel Metropole, the Moscow home of Israel's embassy to the Soviet Union. Golda's tenure in the Soviet Union was brief but significant — her presence elicited a dramatic reawakening of the Russian Jewish population's long-suppressed Jewish identity.

Jews in the Soviet Union had been cut off from the rest of Europe, and from Palestine, since the Russian Revolution of 1917 that overthrew the tsarist aristocracy. In the new, communist state that assumed power, worship of any religion was banned, and Judaism in particular came in for sometimes brutal persecution. Jewish studies were forbidden, as were the celebration of Jewish holidays, the baking of matzoh at Passover, and other rituals central to Jewish life. The authorities boasted that all of Russia's Jews had been assimilated

— that is, had their "Jewishness" absorbed by the larger identity of being a Soviet citizen.

Shortly after Golda took up her post as ambassador, Jews celebrated the "High Holy Days" — Rosh Hashanah, the New Year, and Yom Kippur, the Day of Atonement. A few days before Rosh Hashanah, an article in *Pravda*, the Communist Party newspaper, stated that "the state of Israel has nothing to do with the Jews of the Soviet Union." Many Jews, accustomed to reading "between the lines" of official pronouncements, took this as a veiled warning to stay away from Golda and her delegation from Israel. They did exactly the opposite.

New Year's services at Moscow's Great Synagogue brought an extraordinary showing of Russian Jews — the crowd has been estimated at anywhere from 30,000 to 50,000 people. Just weeks before, Golda had been to Sabbath services and seen only a hundred or so in attendance.

"I couldn't grasp what had happened — or even who they were," Golda wrote of her surprise. "And then it dawned on me. They had come . . . in order to be with us, to demonstrate their sense of kinship and to celebrate the establishment of the State of Israel."

Golda found herself in the middle of this incredible throng. Thousands of Russian Jews pressed close to see her, to touch her. All the while they repeated, "Nasha Golda, Shalom. Nasha Golda, Shalom," a greeting which meant "Our Golda, Peace."

"I wanted to say something, anything, to those people," Golda remembered. "To let them know that I begged their forgiveness for not having wanted to come to Moscow and for not having known the strength of their ties to us."

"Thank you for having remained Jews," she told the crowd. Her words were passed from person to person. Back at the hotel after services, the ambassador and her colleagues could do nothing but sit in silence, flooded with emotion.

A few days later, services for Yom Kippur produced a similar scene. It was these experiences — and the hope they embodied — that made Golda feel her time in Moscow had been worthwhile. Ultimately, however, it would be decades before the Soviet government allowed Jews to worship freely or emigrate to Israel. Reforms carried out in the late 1980s under the leadership of Mikhail Gorbachev led to a dramatic increase in the number of Russian Jews going to Israel.

In January 1949, Golda was elected to the first Knesset, or Parliament, as a member of the Mapai or Israel Workers Party, which was headed by David Ben-Gurion. Ben-Gurion wanted her to serve as Minister of Labor in his government, and summoned her home from Moscow in March to be sworn in. She returned to Israel to take up her post and the task she knew best — building a new nation.

Her new position was everything she had worked toward. Golda had twice been an immigrant — first to America, then to Palestine — and she knew the troubles people faced in a new land. She had been poor, and had experienced firsthand the difficulty in surviving with very few resources. And she was a socialist, committed to justice and equality for all. The new state of Israel presented a clean slate on which to build and fulfill these ideals. Indeed, Golda's entire life seemed to have prepared her for this very position.

The most pressing problem facing the new state was that of immigration. The "ingathering of exiles" that marked Israel's first few years meant that literally hundreds of thousands of Jews from around the world arrived in the country. Between January 1919 and May 1948, the period of the British Mandate, about 390,000 Jews had come to Palestine. In the first year of the state, there were almost 685,000 newcomers. By the end of 1949, Jews were streaming in at a rate of about 1,000 a day.

They came from Turkey, Poland, Rumania, Germany, Austria, Italy, Cyprus, China, India, and elsewhere. Between December 1948 and September 1950, "Operation Magic Carpet" airlifted nearly 50,000 Yemenite Jews to Israel. Most of them had lived in poverty and despair for generations. Some had never even seen an airplane before, and had heard only a little about the Jews' return to the Holy Land.

Some Jews thought that restrictions ought to be placed upon immigration, since the huge waves of newcomers meant rationing and austerity for those already in Israel. Golda believed that any such limits would be a complete contradiction of every principle upon which the new nation was founded and that Israel should be a haven for Jews from everywhere. Indeed, one of Israel's fundamental laws is the Law of Return, which guarantees automatic Israeli citizenship to all Jewish immigrants as soon as they step foot on Israeli soil.

Each of these new citizens needed to be housed, fed, and clothed, and to be given jobs. Their children needed schools and medical care. There needed to be some mechanism for having them get along with each other, despite their wildly different backgrounds and life-styles. It was a monumental task even for a large and wealthy nation. For a small state such as Israel, it was an incredible challenge. The country was still officially at war with its neighbors, and had to support a large army. And there wasn't any room for half-measures. Everything had to be done at once.

It was Golda's job to get things done.

Throughout the early to mid-1950s, it was Golda who visited the new immigrants in their tent villages, the camps where they stayed after arriving in the country. It was Golda who set up the training programs so that these immigrants learned skills for jobs. It was Golda who initiated large-scale housing and road building projects — apartments, groceries, synagogues, and schools. It was Golda who ordered expensive design changes so that housewives would have windows in the kitchens in which they spent much of their time. It was Golda who made sure that teams of public workers were ethnically mixed so that a new society of Israelis began to form.

Golda designed Israel's national health insurance plan. She had the idea to sell State of Israel Bonds in foreign countries to raise more money. As a result, some three billion dollars made its way to Israel over the next twenty years. She journeyed to the United States to drum up support — and found backing from President Truman.

Golda seemed to be everywhere at once. She found herself under constant attack for spending too much of the nation's money, but she was not deterred. "Without doubt," she later wrote, these years were "the most satisfying, the happiest in my life."

The one place Golda wasn't in all these years was with Morris. Her children were grown and on their own. Menachem, influenced by his father's love of music, had become a professional cellist. Sarah, more like her mother, was living on Kibbutz Revivim. Golda's parents had moved to Palestine in 1926.

Morris and Golda had officially separated in 1938, and in 1951 Morris died. Golda flew home from one of her trips abroad for the funeral, and later in life spoke movingly about their relationship.

"He came to Israel because I wanted to come to Israel. He came to the kibbutz because I wanted to be on a kibbutz. He took up a way of life that didn't suit him because it was the kind of life that I couldn't do without . . . . It was a tragedy. A great tragedy. Because, as I say, he was a wonderful person and with a different woman he could have been very happy."

Morris put things more simply. "I came to Palestine to be with Golda, but Golda wasn't there."

But if in life Golda had had little time to think about Morris, after his death she had even less. The difficult issues confronting Israel were foremost in her mind. Among these was the nation's response to Arab acts of aggression — the terrorist attacks launched across the borders that frequently took Jewish life and property.

Ben-Gurion favored strong, forceful retaliation — striking back against the terrorist without mercy. He was less concerned with what world opinion might say. He felt that the Israeli citizen had a right to feel secure in his own state. Foreign Minister Moshe Sharett, on the other hand, was more concerned with the criticism that was heaped upon Israel when it attacked the terrorists in turn. He did not want tiny Israel to become isolated, to find itself without friends among other countries.

Prime Minister Ben-Gurion grew less and less tolerant of his foreign minister's attitude. The two even had open disputes at cabinet meetings. Golda sided with Ben-Gurion, not for political reasons but because she, too, felt militant about making sure the Arabs knew that terrorism had its price. It was an attitude that set the stage for her next move up the government ladder.

In 1956, Ben-Gurion, Sharett, and others were discussing the future of the Mapai Party. The prime minister felt the party was in need of rejuvenation. When Sharett joked that perhaps *he* should become Mapai's new secretary-general, the party's leading post, Ben-Gurion leaped at the opening.

"Marvelous," he said. "A wonderful idea! It will save Mapai." Sharett was furious at Ben-Gurion's crafty maneuver to remove him from the foreign ministry. But he had no choice but to obey.

Several days later, Golda was speaking with Ben-Gurion about this new development. "But who will be foreign minister?" she asked him.

"You," he replied. "That's that."

And it was. Golda was about to step onto the world stage.

9

On the World Stage

AFTER GOLDA BECAME foreign minister, she changed her last name from her married name of Meyerson, to Meir. Ben-Gurion told all his cabinet ministers that he wanted them to take Hebrew last names — as many Jewish immigrants in Israel did. Golda decided she wanted to use a Hebrew word that sounded almost the same as the name she'd been using since she was a young woman. She chose "Meir," which means "to illuminate."

Not everyone agreed with Ben-Gurion's choice of Golda Meir as foreign minister. Much of the public saw her as a strange sort of leader — half grandmother, half politician. They also questioned whether she had the experience necessary to handle such a sensitive, visible job.

Golda was someone who prized getting things done. International relations was quite different from nation-building. A good foreign minister had to have the ability to be vague when necessary, and to be patient with an often maddeningly slow pace of progress. Meir was frank, brutally so at times. She was precise, and she liked quick results. How was she going to survive as foreign minister?

Meir herself thought Ben-Gurion wanted to punish her with the foreign minister's post. The Labor Ministry was the best place for her, she thought. In her view, foreign ministers did nothing but talk. Once again, though, it was her duty, and she took up the job with typical zeal. First, Meir gave strong support to the prime minister's policy of swift retaliation against Arab attacks, something that Sharett had been unwilling to do. This pleased Ben-Gurion, and even led him to say on one occasion that Meir was "the only man in my cabinet."

This comment angered Meir. She did not appreciate Ben-Gurion's jokes about conventional male-female roles. She was one of the world's most prominent politicians. Women the world over looked to her for inspiration. Yet Golda was not a feminist in the conventional sense. As she once told an interviewer, "I've lived and worked among men all my life, and yet to me the fact of being a woman has never . . . been an obstacle. It's never made me uncomfortable or given me an inferiority complex. Men have always been good to me . . . . Men have never given me special treatment but neither have they put obstacles in my way."

On at least one count, however, Meir did agree with the philosophy of what would later be called the women's liberation movement: "I agree [that] to be successful, a woman has to be much more capable than a man. Whether she dedicates herself to a profession or dedicates herself to politics."

Meir didn't have to wait long to face her first crisis

as foreign minister. Tensions between Israel and its Arab neighbors escalated in 1955. In September, Egypt's President Gamal Abdal Nasser sent his navy to blockade the Straits of Tiran in the Red Sea. One of Israel's major shipping routes was cut off. Nasser also entered into a pact with Czechoslovakia by which Egypt would obtain far more arms than it needed for self defense — thus posing a direct threat to Israel.

Then, on July 26, 1956, President Nasser stunned the world by nationalizing the Suez Canal, the vital waterway linking the Mediterranean Sea with the Indian Ocean. Nasser's move jeopardized the free passage through the canal that ships from all countries relied on. France was already at odds with Nasser for his support of anti-French rebels in Algeria, where France ruled as a colonial power. By late October, Egypt had formed a joint military command with Syria and Jordan, and war looked inevitable.

France and England wanted to stop Nasser through military intervention. Israel had recently concluded several arms deals with France, and had close contacts with the French military. Shimon Peres, the director-general of Israel's defense ministry, was in Paris shortly after Nasser seized the Suez Canal. He was approached by France's defense minister.

"How much time do you think would it take for your army to cross the Sinai peninsula and reach the Suez?" Peres was asked. It was a simple question. What followed was something much more complex — the Sinai Campaign.

Over the next few weeks, Ben-Gurion, Peres, Meir, and Moshe Dayan, a maverick soldier who three years earlier had become the army's chief of staff, made frequent trips to Paris for secret talks. A plan was drawn up. Israeli troops, supported by French and British paratroopers, would attack and seize the region. Total secrecy was the order of the day. Indeed, Golda was one of only ten people who knew of the planned assault.

On the day of the attack, Israel easily defeated the Egyptians and put them on the run. But when the fighting came to a halt, Israel came under strong pressure from the United Nations and from U.S. President Dwight D. Eisenhower to withdraw. Israel said it would comply, but only when it was satisfied with security arrangements in Sinai. Finally, in March 1957, Meir went before the UN to make the painful announcement that Israel would pull its soldiers out of Egyptian territory.

Golda described it as a "heart-breaking" diplomatic battle. The four-and-a-half months of negotiations had taught her much about international diplomacy. For one thing, she learned that too many diplomats made promises without ever intending to follow through on them. She agreed with many of her fellow Israelis, who said that the next time they occupied territory as a result of a defensive war, they would withdraw only in exchange for a treaty of peace.

As for the Arabs, Golda was angered by their willingness to make war, but not to negotiate for peace. Despite Golda's belief in forceful retaliation, she truly wanted peace and was disappointed that the Arabs did not. She felt compelled to end her speech to the UN with these words:

"Now may I add these few words to the states in the Middle East area and, more specifically, to the neighbors of Israel? Can we from now on, all of us, turn a new leaf, and instead of fighting among each other can we all, united, fight poverty, disease, illiteracy? Can we, is it possible for us to pool all our efforts, all our energy, for one single purpose — the betterment and progress and development of all our lands and all our peoples?"

Meir represented her country at another difficult UN session in 1960. Israeli Nazi-hunters had tracked down Adolf Eichmann, who was living in hiding in Argentina. Eichmann was a war criminal, the man who carried out Hitler's "final solution," to kill all the Jews in the world. Israeli secret agents kidnapped Eichmann and brought him back to Israel to stand trial. Argentina was outraged at this violation of its sovereignty, and sought UN help in obtaining Eichmann's return. Meir faced the daunting task of arguing against the request — even though that meant condoning acts such as kidnapping that some people called illegal.

Golda later called the address she delivered "the one that most drained me, because I felt I was speaking for millions who could no longer speak for themselves and I wanted each word to have meaning."

Meir's defense of the Israeli action was based on her view that Eichmann, living in freedom and without being punished for his terrible war crimes, was a greater menace than honoring certain laws. The UN agreed — in part. The Security Council passed a resolution condemning Israel's act. Israel expressed its regret. This seemed to satisfy Argentina's complaint. Then the United Nations Security Council also expressed its opinion that Eichmann be brought to trial — and he was, in Israel.

The trial, broadcast live over the radio, featured graphic testimony about the Nazi death camps. Many wondered how Israelis managed to endure hearing about the concentration camps once again, and the awful things that had happened there. In fact, the trial helped Israelis come to terms with this horrible chapter in Jewish history.

For one thing, the Jews now had Israel, a state of their own, which gave them a sense of security they had not had before. The trial enabled survivors to impress on succeeding generations the belief that such a horror should never be allowed to happen again. And the fact that a leading Nazi was being tried for his crimes did much to restore a belief in justice. In 1962, Eichmann was convicted of having played a major role in the murder of millions of Jews. He was sentenced to death, and hanged.

In answer to those who thought the Israelis had exacted revenge and nothing more, Golda wrote in her autobiography, "The trial of Adolf Eichmann [was] a great and necessary act of historic justice . . . . It was not, in any sense, a question of revenge. As the Hebrew poet Bialik once wrote, not even the devil himself could dream up an adequate revenge for the death of a single child, but those who remained alive — and generations still unborn — deserve, if nothing else, that the world know in all its dreadful detail, what was done to the Jews of Europe and by whom."

Meir's most visible effort as her country's foreign minister was the hand of friendship she extended to the newly independent countries of Africa. Golda offered these nations the wisdom of what Israel had learned in its first decade. While the superpowers offered money and machinery, Golda decided to offer something different — people.

Israeli doctors, teachers, engineers, farmers, and others traveled to all parts of Africa as part of Meir's diplomatic initiative. In turn, Africans were invited to study at Israel's technical schools and universities. They were able to see for themselves the kibbutzim and factories that made Israel work.

Meir's forthrightness won Israel many much-needed friends on the African continent. In 1964, during a trip to Zambia for that country's independence celebration, Golda was invited to visit the spectacular Victoria Falls in neighboring Rhodesia. At that time, Rhodesia was a ruled by white people, who discriminated against the many black people in their own country. When Golda's delegation reached the border, they were asked to form separate lines for blacks and whites to have their passports looked at.

Golda was offended by such blatant discrimination. "I can do without the Falls," she announced, turning back.

By the end of Meir's service as foreign minister, such honesty had performed wonders. The number of Israeli diplomatic missions in Africa had grown from one to thirty. Meir herself had traveled some 100,000 miles there, and in the process became the best-known white woman in Africa.

Eventually, however, African countries developed close relations with the Arab countries. Because of disagreements with Israel over the Israeli occupation of Arab land, many of the nations Meir befriended broke their ties with Israel. Today, Israel has restored ties with many, but the work Golda set out to do remains unfinished.

In the early 1960s, Meir was also able to strengthen U.S. ties to her country. In 1962, she met with President John F. Kennedy and got him to promise to support Israel if attacked. After Kennedy was assassinated in November 1963, she met with his successor, Lyndon B. Johnson, on the evening of Kennedy's funeral. "I know that you have lost a friend," Johnson told her. "But I hope you understand that I, too, am a friend."

Meir's "friends" at home were suddenly making her life as foreign minister more difficult. Ben-Gurion, seeing how famous his foreign minister was becoming, started taking more trips abroad and getting involved in foreign affairs himself. Policy statements were drafted and issued without Golda's knowledge. For instance, she had not been informed about the plan to capture Eichmann until after Ben-Gurion had given it his approval.

In addition, Shimon Peres was also taking on a higher profile in the government, with Ben-Gurion's blessing. Peres was one of the "young guard" in Israeli politics — a new generation of leaders who thought it was time for the leaders of Meir's generation to step aside. The stage was set for a clash between the two generations. It occurred over relations with France.

France remained an ally of Israel's, and Meir had met and impressed French President Charles DeGaulle. Peres had established separate connections with the people in France's Ministry of Defense. As a result, Peres appeared to be cutting in on Golda's territory. A feud began and at times tempers got so hot that Golda contemplated resigning.

But Meir was also one of the leading candidates to succeed Ben-Gurion as prime minister. Ben-Gurion had dominated the country's politics for two decades. Israelis of all political stripes were waiting for him to give some indication as to who he thought could best step into his shoes. Meir and other men and women from Israel's pioneering generation were set against Peres, Dayan, and other younger members of the government.

Golda felt she was best qualified for the job. Then her friendship with Ben-Gurion began to deteriorate. Her dislike for Peres, Dayan, and the others was well known. But these men displayed the verve and daring so admired by Ben-Gurion. In the early 1960s, Meir criticized Ben-Gurion over the Lavon affair, a security operation in Egypt that had been a failure. This and other political developments led Ben-Gurion to resign in 1963.

He was replaced by Levi Eshkol. Though Meir and Eshkol were political allies, Golda had little inclination to serve under Eshkol, thinking herself more than his equal. At the same time, she didn't want to resign, thinking that this would weaken Eshkol and make Ben-Gurion look good. Then personal concerns intervened. In 1963, Golda was diagnosed as having cancer.

Golda's health had never been all that good. She suffered from migraine headaches, and had been treated at one time or another for kidney stones, phlebitis, pneumonia, and a variety of other ailments. She was also exhausted — from years of travel, of political infighting, of life in a stressful situation.

"It wasn't only my health that bothered me. It was

also the need to recharge my emotional batteries that seemed to be running down slightly because I was tired," she wrote. She told Eshkol, "I want to be able to read a book without feeling guilty or to go to a concert on the spur of the moment, and I don't want to see another airport for several years."

In early 1966, at the age of sixty-seven, Golda Meir resigned her job as Israel's foreign minister. Little did she know that she would return to the government within a month for her greatest challenge yet.

10

Prime Minister Meir

GOLDA MEIR'S "RETIREMENT" lasted barely more than a month.

She had never given up her seat in the Knesset — the Israeli parliament — and it wasn't long before her party, the Mapai, called her back into service as secretary general. Ben-Gurion had bolted the party to form his own — known as Rafi — and Mapai was struggling. Meanwhile, Eshkol's quiet, low-key style left many people longing for a return to the days of Ben-Gurion. There was considerable talk that, behind the scenes, Meir was the true power in the Israeli government.

Israel could not have picked a worse time for a leadership crisis. In late May 1967, Egypt's President Nasser again set his country on a path toward war. "We intend to open a general assault against Israel," he stated. "This will be total war. Our basic aim is the destruction of Israel." Israel faced yet another challenge to its existence. How many fights-to-the-death could one small nation handle?

Nasser followed his blood-curdling words with provocative actions. First, he forced the removal of United Nations' peacekeeping forces from the Sinai peninsula, the "buffer zone" between Egypt and Israel where UN troops had been stationed since 1956. Second, he moved weapons and more than 80,000 Egyptian soldiers into the area. Third, as he had done in 1956, he blockaded the Straits of Tiran, Israel's vital shipping link with Asia. Finally, he enlisted much of the Arab world in this latest war campaign, making military alliances with Jordan, Syria, and Iraq.

The primary question facing Israel was whether it should wait for Egypt to strike, or mount a preemptive attack. If Israel chose the former, was it strong enough to absorb the first blow and still hit back with enough force to turn the tide? A preemptive attack would take away the enemy's advantage in personnel and arms, but would leave Israel open to being branded the country that "shot first."

Meir, though no longer part of the cabinet, was called upon to take part in the decision. She and the rest of Israel's leaders felt that war had to be averted. The government sent the new foreign minister, Abba Eban, on a dizzying round of diplomatic missions to London, Paris, and Washington. He returned with the bad news that these governments, friends and allies of Israel, planned no direct action to forestall war. Israel was on its own.

There was no choice but to order a total military mobilization. Ordinary daily life in Israel was over, at least temporarily. Buses normally used for commuters were instead used for military transport. Public parks were blessed by rabbis for use as emergency cemeteries.

Shortly after seven a.m. on June 5, 1967, Israeli warplanes swung out over the Mediterranean and entered Egyptian air space, flying low to avoid radar detection. With lightning speed and remarkable accuracy, they destroyed most of Egypt's entire air force — more than 300 warplanes — on the ground. Meanwhile, on the ground, the Israeli army advanced on all fronts, into Syria, Jordan, and the Sinai. Planes, tanks, and infantry achieved similar success. Once again, Israel's enemies had been defeated. Within days, the magnitude of an astonishing military victory had become clear.

From Egypt, Israel captured the Sinai and Gaza Strip. From Syria, Israel wrested the Golan Heights. And from Jordan, Israel seized the West Bank and East Jerusalem. In just six days, Israel had overwhelmed the Arabs. It was one of the greatest military triumphs in history. Historians, journalists, and the general public alike ran out of glowing words to describe what had happened. It was, they agreed, a victory of almost biblical and mythical proportions.

Like many of her countrymen, Golda visited the Western Wall in Jerusalem quickly after the capture of the Old City. The Wall was all that remained of the huge Second Temple complex that had been destroyed in the first century A.D., and was Judaism's holiest shrine. Tradition held that written messages left between the cracks of the stones carried religious weight. Meir scribbled a prayer for peace and followed the ancient custom. Then, on the last day of the war, she traveled to New York, honoring a commitment she had made prior to the outbreak of hostilities.

Speaking at rally after rally, she found American Jewry in a state of euphoria equal to that of the Israelis. She was especially moved by those Americans who had tried to come to Israel to join their fellow Jews in battle. Meir described this impulse in her autobiography.

"The threat we were experiencing . . . was the threat of extinction, and to that Jews respond in the same way, whether they go to synagogue or not, whether they live in New York, Buenos Aires, Paris, Moscow, or Petach Tikvah. It is a deeply familiar threat, and when Nasser and his associates made it, they doomed their war to failure because we had decided — all of us — that there was to be no repetition of Hitler's 'Final Solution,' no second Holocaust."

Meir's role in the Six-Day War had been relatively small, especially compared to that of Defense Minister Moshe Dayan, who spearheaded Israel's military machine. But in the winter following the war, Golda engineered the creation of a new political force — Israel's United Labor Party.

The formation of the Labor Party grew out of Golda's conviction that Israel's workers' parties needed to end their squabbling if people were to vote for them and elect them as the government. The Mapai Party had been jolted by the defection of Ben-Gurion in 1965. He had left, along with Dayan, Peres, and others, to form his own party. Ahdut Avodah was yet another party competing for voters' attention.

Meir convinced the leaders of the three parties to form an alliance, and she was named its secretary general. She had not, however, brought the federation into being for her own advancement. To the contrary, in July 1968, having completed this task, she resigned yet again. Seventy years old and worn out by the infighting, she looked forward to giving herself a much needed rest. Yet once more she was called back into government service.

On February 26, 1969, Prime Minister Levi Eshkol suffered a fatal heart attack. Jockeying to succeed him were Dayan, hero of the Six-Day War, and Yigal Allon, another prominent military figure and politician. Neither the government nor the public wanted to see a political tug-of-war. Golda's decisiveness was a clear asset in this regard.

In addition, Arab shelling of Israel's border regions had become more and more frequent, raising again the specter of war. Golda's proven willingness to be "tough" with Arab aggression also added to her support. It wasn't long before she emerged as the compromise choice to serve as prime minister until the general elections scheduled for October.

On March 7, Meir was appointed prime minister after a vote of confidence by the Labor Party's central committee. Weeping openly as the voting results were announced, she told her party colleagues that she was "not sure I will succeed." She also wasn't sure she wanted the job. For one thing, she was old. For another, it was apparently only a temporary position until the people could elect a new leader. The crowd, as if to disagree with this assessment, responded with chants of "Golda! Golda!"

Ten days later, the full Knesset followed suit. Again

Meir expressed grave reservations about her ability to do the job. "I was dazed," she later recalled. "I . . . knew that now I would have to make decisions every day that would affect the lives of millions of people . . . But there wasn't much time for reflection, and any thoughts I had about the path that had begun in Kiev and led me to the prime minister's office in Jerusalem had to wait."

Golda Meir was sworn in, becoming just one of three women prime ministers in the world. But Meir's reservations about the job were mirrored by those of the public. The authoritative Israeli newspaper, *Ha'aretz*, voiced one concern: "The people of Israel have the right to expect that the helm will be given to a younger person, whose power of action will not be restricted by age or health."

Undeterred, Golda settled into office, ready to confront the issues. She found no shortage of those. For the next five years, she was to be almost entirely preoccupied with continued Arab hostility toward Israel.

Golda Meir had a distinct style as prime minister, Always seen by the Israeli public as something of a grandmother, she played the role with her cabinet colleagues as well. Regular cabinet meetings were held on Sundays. On Saturday nights, Meir would host an intimate gathering of her closest advisers, who would dine on Golda's home cooking while they enjoyed freewheeling discussions, and a frank exchange of opinions and ideas. Meir was often accused of "cooking up" more than just chicken soup. Critics felt she used the Saturday night gatherings to circumvent the cabinet's normal decision-making process.

She also had erratic sleeping habits. She didn't need

much sleep, in any case, and frequently stayed up late with advisers or simply pondering over a decision. Often she would surprise soldiers guarding the prime minister's residence by appearing outside to share a three a.m. cigarette. Golda had one bad habit — she was a chain smoker.

The most immediate crisis facing the new prime minister was the threat of war from Egypt. Some Israelis thought that the one-sided results of the Six-Day War would lead the Arabs to realize, once and for all, that Israel was in the Middle East to stay. Perhaps now they would make peace. But they were wrong.

In August 1967, the Arabs, meeting in Khartoum, Sudan, had issued the "three no's" — no peace, no recognition of the state of Israel, no negotiations. In 1969, that policy had not changed.

President Nasser of Egypt changed his tactics. Instead of outright war, which he could not win, Nasser mounted a "war of attrition." Using arms it had received from the Soviet Union, Egypt began a steady barrage of artillery attacks across the Suez Canal. These were aimed at Israeli shipping and other military or commercial targets.

Though Israel had few population centers near the canal zone, Israel paid a heavy price from the shelling. By August 1970, when a cease-fire was put in place, 721 Israelis had been killed. This was just 69 less than had died in the entire Six-Day War.

Throughout the war of attrition, and throughout talks with the United States, which had become involved in negotiating a truce, Meir paid the Egyptians in kind. One Israeli bombing mission carried out in retaliation forced the evacuation of tens of thousands of people from Egyptian cities near the canal. "We can take more than [the Arabs] believe we can take," she stated. "And we can fight back."

There was no arguing with the fact that the borders Israel had established with its victory in 1967 left it more secure, in military terms, than it had been before. But there are many aspects to security. In the flush of the amazing 1967 victory, at least one of those facets was overlooked. What was Israel to do about the enormous Arab population — numbering about one million people — that lived in the "occupied territories" of the West Bank and Gaza Strip? Suddenly Israel found itself responsible for all these people.

Some Jews called for the area's annexation. They felt a spiritual, religious link to the land of their biblical forefathers. They even believed that their God had played a hand in the region's having fallen into Israeli hands. Shortly after the 1967 war, zealots began creating Israeli settlements in the area as a way of staking a permanent claim on the land. They were supported, on and off, by the government.

Most Israelis, however, saw the area as a bargaining chip. The occupied territories could be returned to the Arabs in exchange for a peace treaty. "As long as there is no peace agreement between us and our Arab neighbors," stated Golda, "we stand where we are."

At the same time, however, the national aspirations of the Palestinians in the occupied territories grew more pronounced. They felt that their claim on the land was every bit as legitimate as that of the Jews, and wanted a state of their own, with East Jerusalem as its capital.

Many Israelis had a difficult time accepting this point of view, even though the Palestinian Arabs' yearning for a homeland seemed to mirror the Jews' own struggle for statehood.

Many Israelis tried to downplay the Palestinian aspirations. Golda Meir even went so far as to say, in a 1969 interview, "It was not as though there was a Palestinian people and we came and threw them out and took their country away from them. They did not exist."

The statement sparked an outcry. Many felt it unduly harsh. Others thought it historically wrong. Still others thought it was a blunder to try to deny the existence of the Palestinian people. However it was interpreted, it didn't do very much for Israel's image in the eyes of a world anxious for a peace settlement.

It may also have served as a rallying cry for a new player in the field of Palestinian politics — the Palestine Liberation Organization. The PLO rejected negotiation with Israel and used terrorism to draw attention to the plight of the Palestinian people, those Arabs who had been forced from their homes when Israel was founded in 1948.

Among the PLO's more notorious attacks were the murder of eleven Israeli athletes at the 1972 Olympic Games in West Germany, and an attack on a school in northern Israel in which many Israeli schoolchildren were killed. Though the PLO's tactics horrified Israel's supporters and detractors alike, they served to keep the Palestinian issue near the top of the international agenda.

As prime minister, Golda Meir met with many heads of state, cabinet ministers, ambassadors, and other leading dignitaries and government figures. One of the most historic of these encounters was her meeting with Pope Paul VI in January 1973 — the first time that a Pope had met with an Israeli prime minister. While the symbolism of the meeting was important, Golda Meir had more tangible results in mind for another of her high-level meetings — a series of secret meetings, beginning in 1970, with King Hussein of Jordan.

Hussein was the grandson of King Abdullah, whom Meir had met with twice just before Israel's founding. Abdullah had paid for his peaceful intentions toward the Jews. On July 22, 1951, upon emerging from prayer at Jerusalem's el-Aksa Mosque, he was assassinated. Hussein, as a boy, had witnessed the killing and was commonly said to have absorbed a lesson that day — he who talks peace with the Jews risks his life.

This did not keep him from exploring, with Golda Meir, the prospects for peace. The two leaders met ten times during Meir's tenure as prime minister — in London, Paris, Tel Aviv, and near the Israel-Jordan border near the Israeli town of Eilat. Unfortunately, the talks never produced any breakthrough, though they did give Golda hope that someday such talks would not have to be held in secret.

In April 1973, Golda's doctors determined that her cancer had spread. For ten years she had kept her initial diagnosis a secret from all but her children and a few intimate associates. She had also been able to continue her work unaffected by the illness. Now she would have to undergo several sessions of cobalt radiation treatments, and suffer the side effects. She wondered if she would be able to continue as prime minister. As it turned out, Meir was able to keep to her demanding work schedule, and then some. She even decided to run for re-election in October.

The Labor Party, unaware of her private plight, was pleased with her decision. All the struggles notwithstanding, the situation in Israel, according to some of its leaders, was good. Yitzhak Rabin, Israel's ambassador to the United States until early 1973, had stated that Meir "has better boundaries than King David or King Solomon." Moshe Dayan echoed that sentiment the following month, speaking of "a new state of Israel with broad frontiers, strong and solid, with the authority of the Israel Government extending from the Jordan to the Suez Canal."

Sadly, they were both tragically wrong.

11

The Yom Kippur War

I N MAY 1973, Israel learned that Egypt and Syria had strengthened units of their armies that were located near the front lines of the Suez Canal and Golan Heights. By September, the numbers of those troops had increased dramatically. Israeli military officials were puzzled. What were the Arabs going to do? Did they simply want to defend themselves better against Israeli retaliatory strikes, or were they going to mount yet another attack?

As the build-up became apparent over the summer, Israeli intelligence officers told Meir that the Arabs were not preparing for war. But Meir's instincts told her otherwise. She saw a contradiction between what her experts were telling her, and the situation "on the ground." She remembered, too, that just before the 1967 war, the Arab press was reporting that *Israel* was massing its troops on the borders. This was exactly what the Arab press was saying now.

Still, Golda Meir wasn't sure. "How could it be that I was still so terrified of war breaking out when the present chief-of-staff, two former chiefs-of-staff . . . and the head of intelligence were far from sure that it would? . . . Was I perhaps talking myself into something? I couldn't answer my own questions."

It was the day before Yom Kippur, the Day of Atonement, Judaism's most sacred religious holiday. She wondered whether the country, even in the midst of observing the holiday fast on this, the holiest day of the year, should mobilize its reserves. She herself decided to stay in Tel Aviv rather than join her daughter in Revivim for the holiday fast, as she had planned.

Just before dawn on Yom Kippur, October 6, 1973, information reached Israeli intelligence saying that before sundown, Egypt and Syria would launch a simultaneous attack on Israel. At 7 a.m., Meir convened an emergency meeting to discuss military options. She decided to mobilize 100,000 soldiers. Ironically, Yom Kippur offered almost ideal circumstances for a call-up of Israeli soldiers. Since, for religious reasons, no one drove cars on Yom Kippur, the roads were clear. Had Egypt and Syria selected any other holiday for their surprise attack, chances are the roads would have been crowded with cars headed for the beach!

Later that morning, Meir faced the most important decision of the day — whether or not to order a preemptive air strike. Deciding for an air strike meant going on the offensive. Deciding against one meant that Israel would have to absorb the first blow. Meir decided against the strike, with no objections from the cabinet. She remembered the bitter experiences of Suez and the 1967 war, when Israel had been soundly condemned by other countries for "shooting first." Said Golda, "It has to be crystal clear who began the war, so we won't have to go around the world convincing people our cause is just."

War broke out at 1:55 p.m. on Yom Kippur.

"They'll be sorry for it," were the prime minister's first words when she heard the news. But she was angry with herself, too, for not having ordered a full-scale call-up. It was a mistake for which she never forgave herself.

The war that followed was unlike anything Israel had ever experienced in any of its previous wars. Together, Egypt and Syria had a ten to one advantage in troops, and relied on sophisticated Soviet weapons. They also had the element of surprise. In the opening hours of battle, Israel came perilously close to disaster. Meir, the cabinet, and Israeli military leaders received reports of heavy casualties, and of a failed counterattack.

When Yom Kippur ended, Meir went on television and broke the news to the nation: "We are in no doubt that we shall prevail. But we are also convinced that this renewal of Egyptian and Syrian aggression is an act of madness."

Israelis, remembering the quick sprints of their army through Arab territory in both 1956 and 1967, were stunned, unaccustomed to such bad news. Unknown to the public, Defense Minister Dayan was even advising that Israel pull back to a line east of Suez, which he felt would be easier to defend than the canal itself, where Israeli lines had been broken by Egyptian soldiers. He also counseled a retreat in the Golan Heights, on the border with Syria. Meir, surprised at Dayan's pessimism, overruled him on both counts.

Meir asked the United States for extra arms. To has-

109

In 1973, war began when Israel's neighbors launched a surprise attack on Yom Kippur, which is a Holy Day for religious Jews. Golda Meir, who was Prime Minister, blamed herself when the country was caught off guard. A few weeks later the war was over and Israel was victorious.

ten her request, she instructed Simcha Dinitz, Israel's ambassador, to visit U.S. Secretary of State Henry Kissinger, even though it was three o'clock in the morning. When Dinitz suggested they wait a few hours, Meir replied, "No, don't wait. Wake up Kissinger and tell him what I'm requesting. And tell him I said he'll sleep after war as much as he wants."

Helped by the arms lift, Israel was gradually able to turn the war to its favor. In Sinai, General Ariel Sharon led a dramatic crossing of the Suez Canal, throwing the Egyptian Army into confusion. On the Golan Heights, Israeli troops pushed back early Syrian advances and moved to within artillery range of Damascus, the Syrian capital. A cease-fire ended the fighting on October 24 with the Israelis holding these positions. If they had chosen to, the Israelis could have claimed an overwhelming military victory. But they didn't, for this war — the Yom Kippur War, as it came to be known — had shaken Israelis to the core.

The death toll was enormous, especially for a tiny country. Some 2,400 Israelis had lost their lives. The financial cost, too, was staggering. Roughly $7.4 billion, or as much as Israel's projected gross national product for the entire year. There was a huge psychological price to pay as well. Israelis worried that the Arabs, by inflicting so much damage, had boosted their confidence to the point where they might try again — and soon.

Then Israelis turned inward, looking for explanations. They asked how Israel could have been so unprepared for the attack. They asked how their leaders — Meir and especially Dayan — had allowed Israel to be-

111

come so vulnerable. Many demanded their immediate resignation. Perhaps the most painful question they asked as part of the postwar reckoning was this: What would Israel do now that the image of the "invincible" Israeli had been undermined?

Responsibility for the Yom Kippur War weighed heavily upon Golda Meir. Though she had had her cabinet's support in all her decisions, she still took her country's losses to heart. But her pain was small compared to that of her countrymen who had lost husbands and sons in battle. Many of those citizens heckled Meir when she appeared in public. Golda's popularity plummeted, and it seemed that she was in danger of losing her position of prime minister of Israel.

In November 1973, the Agranat Commission, named after Shimon Agranat, the president of Israel's supreme court, was appointed to investigate the entire conduct of the war. In an early report, both Meir and Dayan were cleared of any wrong-doing. The commission instead placed much of the "blame" for the Yom Kippur military mistakes on the chief of staff of the army. However, many Israelis continued to demand that the prime minister and defense minister be held accountable for the terrible loss of life suffered in the conflict.

On December 31, 1973, Israelis were given a chance to voice their opinion on the war — at the polls. The election had been originally scheduled for October but was postponed because of the war. Voters deserted Labor in significant numbers, but the party retained enough seats to hang on to power. Golda Meir was to form a coalition government with other political parties.

Still, the public remained in an uproar. The turmoil,

political infighting, and anger over the final Agranat report, released in early April, became too much for Golda to bear. One of the leading activists in Jewish history had reached the end of her career. On April 10, 1974, she announced to an shocked gathering at the Knesset, "I have come to the end of the road. It is beyond my strength to continue carrying the burden."

Meir agreed to stay on as head of a caretaker government through early June. Then she gave up her Knesset seat, making her resignation official. She was seventy-six years old, and looked forward to a simple, leisurely retirement. She wanted to read and study Hebrew, the Bible, and literature, and only be consulted as an elder statesperson.

She lived long enough to see remarkable changes in Israel's political landscape. In 1977, the Labor Alignment was voted out of office for the first time in the history of the state. Taking its place was the Likud, a hawkish, right-wing coalition led by former Irgun terrorist Menachem Begin. Commentators likened the electoral results to an "earthquake," a "deluge," and an "electoral storm."

More remarkable still was the peace overture made in 1977 by Egypt's Anwar Sadat, the architect of the 1973 attack. Addressing his country's parliament, Sadat had said: "Israel will be stunned to hear me tell you that I am ready to go to their home, to the Knesset itself, to argue with them, in order to prevent one Egyptian soldier from being wounded. Members of the People's assembly, we have no time to waste."

Begin responded immediately with an invitation for Sadat to come to Jerusalem. Within days of Sadat's his-

toric address, his plane landed at Israel's Ben-Gurion
Airport. Greeting him were his wartime enemies of just
four years earlier — including Meir.

To Golda Meir, Sadat said, "Madame, I have been
waiting to meet you for a long time." To Ariel Sharon,
he said, "I wanted to catch you there" — meaning in
the Sinai during the war. Sharon replied, "I'm glad to
meet you here instead." To General Mordechai Gur,
who warned the nation that Sadat might be using his
visit as a ruse to start a war, Sadat said, "I wasn't
bluffing."

Meir was pleased at the apparent signs of good will,
but bitter, too, that after making so many efforts at
peace, it was her rival who was suddenly center stage
in peace talks. She was also skeptical that both Sadat
and Begin were serious about concluding a peace
treaty.

Sadat was hailed wherever he went. He prayed at the
el-Aksa Mosque and visited Yad Vashem, the Holocaust memorial and museum. Even as he thrilled Israelis with his intelligence and candor, they knew he was
taking a huge gamble. He was the first Arab leader to
break through the Arabs' collective refusal to recognize
Israel's right to exist. Many Arabs, and especially the
Palestinians, regarded Sadat's overture as a betrayal.
There was a real possibility that he would be assassinated.

Sadat spoke to a crowded Knesset and wasted no
time in uttering the words Israelis had waited a very
long time to hear from an Arab leader: "We agree to live
with you in peace and justice. Israel has become an accomplished fact, recognized by the whole world and the

114

superpowers. We welcome you to live among us in peace and security."

Sadat then voiced the Arabs' demand that all lands occupied by Israel in 1967 be returned. Thus was set in motion the incredible series of negotiations that produced the first Arab-Israeli peace treaty.

Meir was not the only one disturbed by the realization that peace talks might have begun earlier. Sadat's journey to Jerusalem elicited much talk among Israelis about why it *hadn't* happened while Meir was prime minister. Was there something about Golda that had prevented it? Had she been too stubborn, an obstacle to peace all along?

Such talk was difficult for Golda to hear. She had given her life to building a humane, strong state of Israel. To be suddenly perceived as someone who was responsible for a war was an insult. Her side of the story deserved a hearing. She decided she would hold a press conference at which she would defend herself. She began to prepare for it.

Then, in October 1978, she was forced to enter Jerusalem's Hadassah Hospital for treatment of spinal pains. Her health failed rapidly. On December 8, 1978, she died. She was eighty years old. In announcing her death to the nation, doctors also let Israelis know for the first time about Golda's fifteen-year battle with cancer.

Four months later, Egypt and Israel signed the Camp David peace treaty, marking an end to thirty years of hostility and, it was hoped, ushering in a new era of peace in the Middle East.

It was not to work out that way. Sadat was assassinated in 1981 by extremists opposed to Egypt's dealings with Israel and the United States. Since then, the two countries have settled into what has been called a "cold peace." The borders are open, and each country's flag flies in the other's capital city, but there is only minimal contact between the governments and people of the two nations.

Meanwhile, in the occupied territories of the West Bank and Gaza Strip, the situation has become bloodier and more difficult in the years since Golda's death. A writer once compared the task of governing these Arabs to "trying to hold on to and control the thrashing tail of an agitated whale." The Palestinian uprising, or *intifada*, has dramatized the Arab struggle. A solution has yet to be found.

And Israel's need for security, for assurances from its neighbors that it may live in the Middle East in peace, also remains unsatisfied. Peace was the motivating force in the life of Golda Meir. As she once said, recalling the days of pogroms in tsarist Russia, "If there is any explanation necessary for the direction which my life has taken, perhaps it is the desire and the determination to save Jewish children from a similar scene and from a similar experience."

Golda Meir brought humanity, warmth, and honesty to the whirlpool of violence that many say characterizes the Middle East. She made it a better place for the millions of Israelis who live there, and served as a role model for Jews, women, and people the world over who admired her talents. Some would say that her work remains unfinished — that it will remain so until a wide-ranging peace settlement is reached between all countries involved in the Middle East conflict. But her efforts

116

helped to build a Jewish nation after two thousand years of exile. And she accomplished much to bring the current generation within sight of an everlasting peace in the Middle East.

SELECTED GLOSSARY OF HEBREW AND YIDDISH TERMS

Ahdut Avodah — an Israeli political party; literally, Union (Ahdut) of Labor (Avodah)

Degania — a derivative of the Hebrew word for "grain"; also the name of the first kibbutz.

eretz — land.

ha'aretz — idiom meaning "the land," or "the land of Israel." Also the name of Israel's most respected newspaper.

Haganah — the primary Jewish security force in pre-state Palestine; upon statehood members of the Haganah were merged into the Israel Defense Forces.

Hashomer — a pre-state Jewish defense organization; "shomer" means guardian or watchman.

Hatikvah — "The Hope," the Jewish national anthem; "tikvah" means hope.

havlagah — restraint; havlagah was the defensive policy of the Haganah.

Histadrut — the Jewish Labor Federation.

Hovevei Zion — the Lovers of Zion; "Hovevei" is Yiddish, a mixture of Hebrew and German.

Irgun — an extremist Zionist military organization that believed in aggression toward the British and Arabs in Palestine; the full name of the organization was Irgun Z'vai Leumi (National Military Organization).

kibbutz/kibbutzim — a communal settlement formed for the sake of settling the land; "kibbutz" is a derivative of the Hebrew word for "group."

Knesset — Israel's Parliament; a derivative of the Hebrew word for "meeting" or "to meet."

Lehi — a short word for Lohamei Herut Israel (Fighters for the Freedom of Israel); another extremist military organization, also known as the Stern Gang, for its founder, Avraham Stern.

Likud — Hebrew for unity; the name of the opposition coalition that came to power as a result of the 1977 elections.

Mapai — for years, Israel's leading political party; the word is an acronym for Hebrew words meaning Israel's Workers Party.

matzoh — the unleavened bread eaten by Jews on Passover, the holiday commemmorating the Jewish exodus from Egypt in biblical times; the Jews ate unleavened bread because, in a hurry to leave, they had no time to add yeast to their bread and wait for the bread to rise.

Nachshon — the name of the first Israelite to jump into the parted waters of the Red Sea during the exodus from Egypt, and the name given to the shipping enterprise started by the Histadrut in the 1930s.

Poale Zion — "Workers of Zion"; "poale" is Yiddish, a mixture of Hebrew and German.

Rafi — the political party formed by David Ben-Gurion when he defected from Mapai; the word is an acronym for Hebrew words meaning Israel Labor List.

Rosh Hashanah — literally, head (rosh) of the year (shanah); the Jewish New Year.

Solel Boneh — the building and construction wing of the Histadrut; literally, Pavers (Solel) and Builders (Boneh).

Vaad Hapoel — the Histadrut's executive committee; "Vaad" means council or committee; "Hapoel" means "workers."

Yad Vashem — the Holocaust memorial and museum in Jerusalem; the words come from a biblical phrase meaning "Monument and Memorial"

Yishuv — settlement; the Jewish community in Palestine.

Yom Kippur — the Day of Atonement; the holiest day of the Jewish year.

Zion — the name given in the Old Testament of the Bible to the Jewish city of King David; in common usage, "Zion" came to refer to the Jewish people and the Jewish homeland.

Other books you might enjoy reading

1. Elon, Amos. *The Israelis: Founders and Sons*. Holt, Rinehart, and Winston, 1971.

2. Fallaci, Oriana. *Interview with History*. Houghton Mifflin, 1977.

3. Laqueur, Walter. *A History of Zionism*. Holt, Rinehart, and Winston, 1976.

4. Meir, Golda. *My Life*. Dell Publishing Company, 1976.

5. Meir, Menahem. *My Mother Golda Meir*. Arbor House, 1983.

6. Sachar, Howard M. *A History of Israel*. Alfred A. Knopf, 1976.

7. St. John, Robert et al., eds. Life World Library: *Israel*. Time Inc., 1965.

8. Syrkin, Marie, ed. *A Land of Our Own: An Oral Autobiography by Golda Meir*. G.P. Putnam's Sons, 1973.

About the Author

Richard Amdur is a writer with a continuing interest in the history of Israel, where he lived for more than a year on Kibbutz Tzorah. He is the author of *Menachem Begin*, *Moshe Dayan*, and *Chaim Weizmann* in the Chelsea House series "World Leaders — Past and Present."